FLYING SCOTSMAN

Written, photographed, compiled and edited by Brian Sharpe
Editorial Assistant: Jeff Colledge
Design: Anita Tams-Waters
Production Editor: Richard Gibson
Advertising: Olivia Taylor-Watson
Publishing Director: Malcolm Wheeler
Finance Director: Brian V Hill
Managing Director: Terry Clark

Additional contributions and photographs supplied with grateful thanks by: Geoff Courtney, Geoff Silcock, Keith Langston, National Railway Museum, Rail Archive Stephenson, Paul Chancellor Collection and Colour-Rail.

Published by
Mortons Media Gr
Media Centre, Morton Way,
Horncastle, Lincolnshire LN9 6JR
Tel: 01507 523456.

Printed by
William Gibbons and Son, Wolverhampton

Published October 2005

ISBN 0-9550221-1-8

mORTONS
Media Group Ltd
Independent publishers since 1885

FLYING SCOTSMAN

Why is this the best-known steam engine in the world?

No 1472 was the third of a class of steam locomotives that was eventually to number 79 engines, and did not originally even carry a name. The Great Northern Railway A1 4-6-2, though, was the biggest express steam engine ever to have been seen in Britain at the time. It was No 1472 that was chosen to be displayed at a major exhibition at Wembley in 1924, and for this it was given the name *Flying Scotsman*.

It hauled the London & North Eastern Railway's first King's Cross-to-Edinburgh non-stop express in 1928, but was beaten by a slightly longer Euston-to-Glasgow non-stop run by the London Midland & Scottish Railway's Pacific No 6201 *Princess Elizabeth* in 1936. It officially broke the 100mph barrier in 1934 but unofficially this speed had been achieved 30 years earlier. An identical engine to *Flying Scotsman* soon eclipsed its speed record with a 108mph burst of speed in 1935.

Flying Scotsman was perhaps becoming the best-known of the class of 79 LNER A1s, but none of its record feats actually stood for long. In 1935, the A1s were superseded by the A4s, streamlined engines with more speed and power, and these raised the speed record first to 112mph, and soon to 126mph.

From then on, *Flying Scotsman* was just one of many engines that played a vital part in hauling East Coast Main Line expresses between King's Cross, the north and Scotland, for another 30 years, but it had no more claim to fame than any of the others.

It still had its name, though, and, when the final curtain came in early 1963 and the engine was withdrawn from service by British Railways and expected to be scrapped, it was purchased by a businessman who had every intention of keeping the engine running.

Flying Scotsman certainly had claims to fame from the early years of its main line career, but it was 1963 when it really started to hit the headlines – after it had retired. This might not have happened had the engine not had such a memorable name.

Flying Scotsman has now become the one steam engine in the world of which everyone knows the name, and which most people would even recognise. It was briefly the only main line steam engine running in the whole of Britain, and it has travelled across the Atlantic and across America. It has circumnavigated the globe,

steamed across Australia, broken the record for a non-stop run with steam (again), and been sold for easily the highest price ever paid for a steam engine.

But it has had its down side, too. It has had several owners, some of whom have bought it on the strength of its earnings potential, based on the name *Flying Scotsman*. This value has perhaps been overestimated, and two of *Flying Scotsman*'s one-time owners have been bankrupted.

It has been said that *Flying Scotsman*'s fame is such that it should have been preserved by the nation anyway. A large number of steam engines was preserved 'officially' and many are now on display in the National Railway Museum at York, but *Flying Scotsman* was simply not considered unique or historically important enough at the time. The streamlined A4 Pacific No 4468 *Mallard* was chosen, along with Gresley's V2 2-6-2 No 4771 *Green Arrow*. *Flying Scotsman* was not sufficiently different from these two to justify its preservation.

Now, of course, its ongoing 40 years of fame (if not fortune) has earned it a place in the National Railway Museum collection and, after an unprecedented fund-raising campaign and a National Heritage Memorial Fund grant, the museum was able to clear the enormous debts of the engine's owning company and acquire *Flying Scotsman* for the nation, and for a British public who clearly hold the engines in high esteem.

If it had not acquired fame, largely as a result of its name, in the 1920s and 1930s, then maybe Alan Pegler would not have had the enthusiasm to purchase it in 1963. If it had been scrapped, what would then have become Britain's most famous steam engine?

The question is asked whether *Flying Scotsman* can run for ever. The answer is probably yes, at a price. Like any steam engine, it is a mechanical object, built of steel. As parts wear out they are replaced. Little of the original engine now exists and there has been much rebuilding and improvement carried out, before and after 1963.

The legend that is *Flying Scotsman* can run for ever; it will be apple green, numbered 4472, carry the famous name and be recognisable as the ultimate in British express steam design elegance. It may not be all the original steel, but the legend that is *Flying Scotsman* goes far beyond its physical characteristics.

LNER A3 Pacific No 4472 *Flying Scotsman* departs from Chinley and takes the Hope Valley line to Sheffield at Chinley North Junction with an enthusiasts' railtour to York on 29 September 1979. BRIAN SHARPE

THE GREAT
Northern Railway

Britain's railway system was built by numerous independent companies, many of which were to amalgamate into larger organisations bearing the well-known names of the late 19th century. These independent companies were to last until 1923, when the 'Grouping' was to form the 'Big Four'. One of the early railway companies, the Great Northern Railway, had as its aim the building of a railway from London to York, by the shortest possible route. It was relatively late in setting out to achieve this, and other companies' trains were already running between the two cities, but by a very circuitous route through Rugby and Derby.

The Act of Parliament authorising the construction in 1846 actually included two different routes, and the first section to be started was the line from Peterborough to Lincoln via Boston. In 1850 the line south was opened from Peterborough to a temporary London terminus at Maiden Lane, with the better-known King's Cross station, located in a then very disreputable part of London, opening in 1852.

Lincoln to Doncaster via Gainsborough was not completed until 1867 so, for a short period, the GNR's expresses to the north ran via Boston to Lincoln, then over the Manchester Sheffield & Lincolnshire Railway to Doncaster via Retford. So much for the direct route to York!

By the time King's Cross opened, though, the GNR's 'towns line' from Peterborough to Doncaster, via Grantham, Newark and Retford, had been completed.

The GNR never reached York, though; it made it only as far as Askern Junction, just north of Doncaster, from where its trains ran over Lancashire & Yorkshire Railway tracks to Knottingley, then over part of the North Eastern Railway to York.

The Great Northern Railway is known for its main line, as this was the route taken by the Anglo-Scottish expresses, one of which was to become known as the 'Flying Scotsman'. Its expresses also ran to Grimsby on its own East Lincolnshire main line and to York, Leeds, Harrogate, Manchester, Stafford, Liverpool and Yarmouth, partly using other companies' routes. The company also carried very heavy coal traffic south from Yorkshire, much of it later running over the line owned jointly with the Great Eastern Railway from Lincoln to March.

Today, apart from the main line north from King's Cross, little of the 1051 miles of the GNR survives. Most of its Lincolnshire lines closed in 1970, apart from the Skegness branch. The Peterborough-to-Doncaster-via-Lincoln line sees an hourly one-coach train, and branches from the main line still serve Cambridge and Nottingham.

The Great North Eastern Railway Company's electric service from King's Cross to the north and Scotland is recognized as one of Britain's premier express train services, using the original GNR main line as far as Askern Junction, its coaches all bearing the legend 'The Route of the Flying Scotsman'.

Right: The Great Northern Railway's main line ran from King's Cross to Doncaster, with branches to Cambridge, Nottingham, Skegness and Grimsby. The map shows the routes remaining open in 2005, with the Grimsby line and other routes in Linconshire having closed by 1970. Also shown are heritage lines and preservation centres, of which only the Lincolnshire Wolds Railway at Ludborough, near Louth, is located on former Great Northern Railway track.

A map of the present-day railway system, showing the major pre-1923 Grouping railway companies, with heritage lines shown, also with their pre-Grouping origins. The map does not show the position exactly at the Grouping, as there were earlier mergers and takeovers. The Cambrian and Lancashire & Yorkshire Railways are shown separately for example, and not as parts of the GWR and LNWR respectively.

KEY

Light Green	Great Northern Railway
Black	London & North Western Railway North London Railway Cromford & High Peak Railway
Red	Midland Railway London Tilbury & Southend Rly Metropolitan Railway
Blue	Great Eastern Railway Lancashire & Yorkshire Railway
Dark Green	Great Central Railway
Orange	North Eastern Railway
Brown	Great Western Railway Midland & Great Northern Joint Railway
Pink	Smaller independent lines, narrow gauge and miniature lines

Jointly-owned lines shown in the colours of the two railways, except for the South Yorkshire Joint Line, owned by GNR, GCR, NER, MR & LYR, which is shown as red & light green.

How great was the
GREAT NORTHERN?

Britain's first public railway was the Stockton & Darlington. The Liverpool & Manchester moved the story on, but the early independent railways all had one thing in common, they had quite unimaginative names, like the Bristol & Exeter Railway. As they grew bigger though, they coined names like the North Eastern or the Midland, and as they grew even bigger, the prefix 'Great' became popular, with the Great Western being quite an apt description of that railway, while the Great Northern was really a bit of an exaggeration. It was neither great in the way that the GWR covered the whole of western England, nor was it really northern, as its main line to the north ran only as far as just beyond Doncaster.

It was the Great Northern Railway's public relations exaggeration in terms of its name, where the myth actually appeared to be more important than the reality, that really set the scene for the building of the world's most famous steam engine.

Competition was fierce, especially for Anglo-Scottish passenger business in the 19th century. Trains ran from King's Cross, the GNR terminus, and Euston, the LNWR terminus, via the east coast and west coast routes respectively, to Aberdeen. The east coast partners of Great Northern, North Eastern and North British railways, and their west coast opposite numbers, the London & North Western and Caledonian railways staged the 'Races to the North' in 1888 and 1895.

Despite the route being longer and hillier, the west coast alliance won the race both times. But it was the GNR which was the senior partner in the east coast collaboration and, although it was on the losing side, its contribution should not be underestimated. The track on its main line was some of the best in the country. Its engines were among the fastest and most reliable, and its coach designs were adopted as standard for the 'East Coast Joint Stock' fleet which was used on Anglo-Scottish services. Despite the public relations 'spin' its choice of company name implied, the Great Northern was one of Britain's railway companies that rarely gave any of its engines names. Perhaps its best-known 19th century engine, the pioneer Stirling 8ft Single, is simply known as No 1.

Left: GNR Stirling 4-2-2 No 1, in steam at Loughborough on the Great Central Railway in 1981.
BRIAN SHARPE

Oppostie: GNR 1897-built directors' saloon coach No 1283 normally on the Bluebell Railway, but seen on the North Yorkshire Moors Railway in 2005.
BRIAN SHARPE

Herbert Nigel Gresley
ENGINEER

Herbert Nigel Gresley was born on 19 June 1876 at 14 Dublin Street, Edinburgh, one of three children of the Rev Nigel Gresley and his wife, Joanna, whom he had married in 1864.

After leaving Marlborough College, the young Gresley was employed as an apprentice by the London & North Western Railway at Crewe, on his 17th birthday, working under the much-feared Francis Webb. Gresley was described as 'more ponderous than talented' at Crewe, but he was certainly ambitious.

In 1898, he moved on to the Lancashire & Yorkshire Railway, where he first worked in the drawing office. There were unconfirmed reports that, in that year, a Lancashire & Yorkshire Railway steam engine, 4-4-2 No 1352, allegedly exceeded 100mph on a run between Liverpool and Southport. These types of engines were known as 'Highflyers' and the young Gresley certainly seems to have been what modern management jargon refers to as a high flyer himself. In 1900 he was appointed running shed foreman at Blackpool, and soon afterwards promoted to assistant manager at Newton Heath carriage works in Manchester.

Gresley married Ethel Frances Fullagar in 1901, and

in 1902 was promoted again, to works manager at Newton Heath, doubling his £250 annual salary. In 1904 he was promoted again to carriage and wagon superintendent of the Lancashire & Yorkshire Railway in the year that the somewhat more plausible 102.3mph run by the Great Western Railway's 4-4-0 No 3440 *City of Truro* took place on Wellington Bank. Although never totally authenticated, it is generally felt that *City of Truro* at least came very close to achieving 100mph, and was the fastest man-made machine in the world at the time.

The Lancashire & Yorkshire was certainly a well-respected railway, but its trains did not quite have the prestige of the Anglo-Scottish expresses. After an interview with its Chief Mechanical Engineer, HA Ivatt, and on the recommendation of John Aspinall of the LYR, Gresley joined the Great Northern Railway as assistant carriage & wagon superintendent in January 1905.

He quickly made his mark on the GNR. His design of elliptical-roofed, steel-framed and teak-bodied coaches was introduced within a year and became standard for the GNR and for East Coast Joint Stock for the Scottish expresses. The coaches set new standards, many features becoming adopted for coach design for many years to come, and the last ones were still in use on British Railways express trains into the mid-1970s. Gresley's design of coach bogie was to last even longer, being used on Southern Region electric stock that is still in use today.

Gresley's coaches were quickly to replace the four- and six-wheeled clerestory-roofed coaches still in widespread use on the GNR. He also made innovations, such as electric lighting and articulated coaches, first for suburban services, but much later even for express trains.

In 1911, at the age of 35, Gresley succeeded Ivatt as the GNR's locomotive engineer, and the railway industry waited to see whether he would be as forward-thinking and innovative with his locomotive designs as he had been with his carriages. Ivatt was a well-respected engineer, and his engines were good, but at the time they were not the best in Britain. Ivatt had recommended Gresley as his successor, but the GNR board must have had reservations about the

Right: H N Gresley.

appointment of someone so young. Gresley was a confident, self-assured young man, who was ambitious and knew what he wanted.

His early locomotive designs for the Great Northern Railway were traditional but, when he started designing new express engines, they were revolutionary, especially the A1 class Pacifics of 1922. They were big, they were successful and they were noticed, not just by his contemporaries but by the Press and the public. None, of course, came to the attention of the Press and public to quite the same extent as did the third of the A1s, *Flying Scotsman.*

Once in charge of locomotive design on the London & North Eastern Railway in 1923, Gresley could really make his mark. He became acquainted with other locomotive engineers in this country and abroad, and he paid attention to their advice.

Although he designed his own conjugated valve gear for three-cylindered engines, he added details recommended by Holcroft of the South Eastern & Chatham Railway, to really perfect the design.

Churchward of the Great Western was considered top of the pile at the time, and his engineering traditions were continued by Collett. Although he played no direct part in the exchange trials of 1925, Gresley took the results seriously; there was room for improvement in his A1 Pacific design. He took the lessons on board and transformed his own design from a good engine into the best in Britain. Gresley started to become front page news and the name *Flying Scotsman* undoubtedly played its part in making him almost a living legend.

The LNER was never a profitable railway and, although Gresley designed and built a lot of engines, much of his effort had to be directed towards rebuilding and improving older designs. Perhaps it was this that led to some quite radical experiments, such as alternative types of valve gear, booster engines fitted to rear carrying wheels to increase power, and feed-water heaters on top of boilers.

Gresley's assistant was Oliver Bulleid, possibly the most innovative locomotive engineer ever to have practised his trade in Britain, later to achieve fame in his own right on the Southern Railway.

But Gresley continued his big engine policy and followed his Pacifics with a three-cylinder 2-8-2 version for freight service. These were simply too powerful for their own good and could haul coal trains that were so long they brought all the other trains to a standstill until they were out of the way.

Gresley visited America and Germany, and also became friendly with Chapelon, the noted French engineer. He used ideas from these sources to further enhance his designs. Many of the more radical ideas were incorporated into a second three-cylinder 2-8-2 design, the P2, the first one carrying the name *Cock o' the North*, and designed to haul heavy trains on the Edinburgh-to-Aberdeen route. With Lenz poppet valve gear, a feed-water heater, Kylchap double blastpipe and chimney and a semi-streamlined appearance, this was a distinctive engine. It and its classmates, which did not all incorporate the experimental innovations, were again just too big for the line they ran on, but they kept Gresley's name in the headlines.

His most unorthodox experiment was the use of a marine-style water-tube boiler at a pressure of no less than 450psi on his W1 class 4-6-4 No 10000. This was not a success but it was something that a railway somewhere needed to experiment with as it could have totally revolutionised steam locomotive design. At least Gresley was not afraid to try it, while his contemporaries were playing safe with designs that were good, strong, powerful, reliable and economical, but somehow lacked the vision and star quality that only Gresley could produce.

And, of course, during all this time through the late 1920s and early 1930s, the A1 and later A3 Pacifics, with *Flying Scotsman* the undisputed star, were continuing to prove, day-in, day-out, that they were

Above: Gresley teak-bodied coach on the North Yorkshire Moors Railway.
BRIAN SHARPE

Above: *Flying Scotsman*, Gresley's best-known creation.
BRIAN SHARPE

Britain's best steam engines.

The only real improvement to the A3 design hardly incorporated any of Gresley's experiments and innovations; it simply took the proven A3 formula and enlarged it a bit, added a streamlined casing and called itself the A4. These elevated Gresley to the status of superstar.

At one point during the inaugural Press run of the 'Silver Jubilee' to Newcastle, Gresley squeezed through the corridor tender, tapped the driver on the shoulder and asked him to ease off a bit as they had twice touched 112mph. One of the LNER's more senior directors was showing signs of nerves! The driver thought the speed was in the 90s.

The one real innovation on the A4s was the adoption of the Kylchap double blastpipe and chimney on the last few members of the class. It was this that gave No 4468 *Mallard* the ability to travel at 126mph, and put Gresley in the headlines yet again in 1938.

Perhaps the real sign of a great locomotive designer is not what the Press or the public think of him, but what the locomotive crews think, and Gresley probably inspired more loyalty in his drivers and firemen than any other engineer in railway history.

He had moved his office from Doncaster to King's Cross on formation of the LNER, and travelled to work daily by train. He made a point of being in regular

contact with the drivers, and this was a style of management that disappeared after his death in 1941 when another tier of management was introduced.

Gresley's engines in much later years found their way to unlikely places, where they were invariably welcomed despite locomotive crews' reputations for conservatism and loyalty to the types of engine they had been used to for years.

Gresley was awarded the CBE in the First World War for his services to the war effort, and knighted in the King's Birthday Honours in 1936.

In 1937, the 100th Gresley Pacific to be built, No 4498, was named *Sir Nigel Gresley* in a ceremony at Marylebone. The knighthood and the naming of an engine were two honours never previously bestowed on any railway Chief Mechanical Engineer while in office.

Herbert Nigel Gresley was born in 1876, during the reign of Queen Victoria. Patrick Stirling's 8ft Single 4-2-2 No 1 had been running for just a few years, and this is the type of locomotive that would have been familiar to Gresley in his childhood.

Yet Gresley's steam engines were still hauling some of Britain's fastest express trains when Beatlemania hit Britain in 1962. Such was the pace of change in society and on the railways in particular. Gresley's long-lived influence on British social history should not be underestimated.

The locomotive
ENGINEERS

Great Northern Railway chief mechanical engineers

Archibald Sturrock	1850-1866
Patrick Stirling	1866-1895
Henry Alfred Ivatt	1896-1911
Herbert Nigel Gresley	1911-1922

London & North Eastern Railway chief mechanical engineers

Herbert Nigel Gresley	1923-1941
Edward Thompson	1941-1946
AH Peppercorn	1946-1948

Some of Gresley's contemporary chief mechanical engineers in 1911

Great Western Railway:	GJ Churchward	1902-1921
London & South Western Railway:	Dugald Drummond	1895-1912
London & North Western Railway:	CJ Bowen-Cooke	1909-1920
Midland Railway:	Henry Fowler	1909-1922
Great Central Railway	JG Robinson	1900-1922
Great Eastern Railway:	SD Holden	1908-1912
North Eastern Railway:	Sir Vincent Raven	1910-1922
North British Railway:	WP Reid	1903-1919

Locomotive engineers were a breed apart; not only did they tend to move from one railway to another, but many were related by birth and several also became in-laws as marriages took place.

An example is Patrick Stirling. He was the cousin of his predecessor Archibald Sturrock. He had moved from being CME of the Glasgow & South Western Railway; his brother James Stirling also once CME of the GSWR and at one time CME of the South Eastern Railway and Patrick's son Matthew was a long-serving CME on the Hull & Barnsley Railway.

Dugald Drummond joined the London & South Western Railway from being CME of the Caledonian Railway. His brother, Peter, was CME of the Glasgow & South Western Railway.

SD Holden of the Great Eastern Railway was succeeded by his son as CME.

HA Ivatt's eldest daughter married OVS Bulleid, Gresley's assistant on the LNER, who later became CME of the Southern Railway. Meanwhile Ivatt's son became CME of the London Midland & Scottish Railway in 1945.

Edward Thompson, who succeeded Gresley as CME on the LNER, was the son-in-law of Sir Vincent Raven of the North Eastern Railway.

The chief mechanical engineers have tended to be the best-known names from the steam era among railway enthusiasts, far better known, for example, than the railways' chairmen or architects.

The chief mechanical engineers did not physically design their own engines, of course. They relayed the requirements of the management and operating departments to the design staff, and outlined the critical dimensions of the locomotives that were required. The external similarity between the designs of one CME and those of his predecessor arises because the same team of designers would continue under the new leader.

GRESLEY'S
locomotive designs for the GNR

Above: Gresley's third A1 Pacific No 1472 at Doncaster shed soon after construction in 1923. The engine, still unnamed, was allocated here initially and visits to King's Cross were comparatively rare as the Pacifics, with their eight-wheeled tenders, were too long for the turntable.
WH WHITWORTH, RAIL ARCHIVE STEPHENSON

Right: Gresley's first design for the GNR was the H1 2-6-0, later to become LNER K1 and K2 class.

There is no doubt that the GNR had some of Britain's finest 19th century locomotive engineers in charge of designing its engines – Archibald Sturrock, Patrick Stirling and HA Ivatt were all in the premier league.

In 1905, though, Herbert Nigel Gresley joined the company, initially being appointed as carriage and wagon superintendent. The GNR at the time was noted for still running some of the most ancient coaches of any major railway, mostly of six-wheeled design, but Gresley soon changed that.

Having become locomotive engineer in 1911, Gresley's first steam locomotive design for the GNR was the H1 (later LNER K1) 2-6-0 in 1912. They were conventional engines, in traditional GNR style, and designed to accelerate long-distance goods traffic. As early as 1915, though, Gresley was thinking about a four-cylindered Pacific for express trains; unfortunately, wartime was not a good time to build such a thing.

In 1918, Gresley designed the O1 2-8-0 for heavy

Conjugated valve gear

The principle of conjugated valve gear, while not unique or exclusive to Gresley, was only ever used by him in any quantity of steam locomotives produced in Britain. Virtually all of his designs from the O1 2-8-0 onwards used this system, apart from smaller freight and shunting designs.

The valve gear on a steam engine is the complex arrangements of rods that can be seen connecting the cylinders to the driving wheels. It can admit steam to the cylinders at the right time for the engine to move forward or backward, slow or fast. In early engines such as *Locomotion*, it was outside (in fact, above) the engine. Later 19th century designs tended to conceal the valve gear, if not the cylinders, inside, between the frames, for elegance. By the 1920s, though, outside cylinders and valve gear were becoming the norm.

Most engines were, of course, two-cylinder anyway, but three- and even four-cylinder designs started to be adopted, which gave more even power when starting and at speed. In theory, these needed three or four sets of valve gear, with consequent additional weight and maintenance costs. Churchward on the Great Western opted for four cylinders, but used two sets of inside valve gear, controlling two cylinders each.

Gresley chose his three-cylinder design, but with only two sets of valve gear, outside the frames, but connected through the frames, and jointly controlling the inside cylinder.

On a conventional two-cylinder engine, the cranks on the driving wheels are set at 90 degrees to each other, so with each cylinder giving a forward and backward thrust, there are four thrusts at even intervals per revolution of the wheel.

Normally a four-cylinder engine has eight thrusts per revolution, but they are in pairs, so there is no major engineering problem in a set of valve gear controlling two cylinders that act in unison.

A three-cylinder engine, though, has its three cranks set at 120 degrees to each other, so there are six thrusts per revolution. For two sets of valve gear to jointly control a third cylinder so that it acts identically to the one either side, but exactly midway between them, is quite an engineering achievement.

The arrangement had major advantages for smoothness, weight-saving and ease of maintenance, but was still more complex than a conventional two- or four-cylinder arrangement and, with many moving parts between the frames, adequate lubrication was critical. If a Gresley engine ever broke down, it was often caused by problems with the conjugated valve gear between the frames.

freight traffic, and these not only had three cylinders but also Gresley's new design of conjugated valve gear.

This was to set the scene for Gresley's locomotives in the future, but he had yet to build an express engine. Partly this was because Ivatt's Atlantics were so good and were held in such high regard by Gresley that he felt he had little need to improve on them immediately, but it was also because the GNR was in need of more modern freight power.

When Gresley's first express engine did appear, in 1920, the H4 was a 2-6-0 – not a wheel arrangement normally associated with express power, particularly on level tracks. It was built for sustained power output, not high speed, with three cylinders and six small driving wheels, which gave room for a huge boiler. The class was to be reclassified K3 by the LNER and these engines were still pulling summer Saturday expresses to the East Coast in the early 1960s, by which time they were considered rather old and basic medium-sized mixed traffic engines. But when they were built, they were huge express engines that shocked everyone in the railway industry by their sheer size. Gresley was going for big engines, and was not universally popular on the GNR because of what these monsters might do to the track and bridges on the line.

Undeterred, Gresley next went for the biggest engine it was felt possible to build.

Stylistically, the similarity with the H4 (K3) was evident, but it was a 4-6-2, a Pacific, only the second to be built in Britain. The GWR had built the first, called *The Great Bear*, in 1908, and it had proved to be too big to be practical on that railway. Gresley had to compromise with his Pacific design; everywhere weight could be saved, it was, even to the extent of using a lower boiler pressure than would have been ideal. The new engine when it emerged from Doncaster Works in 1922, carrying the number 1470, was considered so important that the GNR even chose to give it a name – *Great Northern*. Partly this was to keep the company

name alive as the GNR was to disappear into the London & North Eastern Railway very shortly. But what had been an imaginative choice of name for the company was really rather less-than-inspiring for the locomotive.

A second engine followed, No 1471. There was no real plan for naming the engines and, after the Grouping in 1923, the LNER turned them out unnamed after naming No 1471 *Sir Frederick Banbury*, but a decision was made to name a third engine for display at the Wembley Exhibition of 1924. No 1472 was named after the GNR's premier express train, the Flying Scotsman. This was a title that had been given unofficially to the GNR's 10am departure from King's Cross to Edinburgh, but was not adopted officially until 1927.

It also happens to sound like a good name for a racehorse, and the town of Doncaster was famous for two things – horseracing and building steam engines.

Left: Gresley's GNR 2-8-0 heavy freight engine.
PAUL CHANCELLOR COLLECTION

GNR
express locomotive development

H A Ivatt's pioneer Atlantic 4-4-2 No 990 *Henry Oakley* at Boston in 1998 (right). No 990 was the first engine of this wheel arrangement to run in Britain and it reversed most of Stirling's design principles. The small cylinders actually result in No 990 being theoretically less powerful than Stirling's No 1, but the extra wheels made the engine much better at starting heavy trains and the much bigger boiler meant it was able to maintain its power for much longer. Externally, though, many of the GNR's design principles were continued, with No 990 still having the same flowing lines in the footplate and an overall tidy and sleek appearance. Ivatt's large Atlantics followed, an equally graceful but much bigger design. Photo by Brian Sharpe.

Patrick Stirling's 4-2-2 No 1 (left). Although the 'single-wheeler' was used by many of Britain's pre-Grouping railways, it was Patrick Stirling of the GNR who took the concept to its ultimate form. These were remarkably powerful engines for their size and could haul trains of 90 to 100 tons from Grantham to King's Cross in two hours. In theory, speed was limited to 60mph on the Great Northern, in common with most railways at the time, but one of Stirling's engines, a 2-2-2, is known to have reached 86mph. Withdrawn and preserved by the Great Northern Railway itself in 1907, No 1 was steamed again by the LNER in 1938, and by the National Railway Museum in 1981. It is seen on the Great Central Railway at Loughborough in May 1982. Photo by Brian Sharpe.

A3 4-6-2 No 4472 *Flying Scotsman* (left) at Carnforth. Although changed in appearance in more recent years, the Pacific design when new in 1922 still continued the GNR tradition of compact and graceful design. Gresley's engines proved to be some of the fastest ever, but they were also powerful for their size when compared to later and bigger British Pacifics. Despite its size, *Flying Scotsman* still has the flowing footplate inherited from Stirling's 8ft Single, as well as many other design features, often considered to be among the best in British steam locomotive design practice. Photo by Jeff Colledge.

Above: Stephenson's Rocket was an 0-2-2 wheel arrangement, with the bare minimum number of wheels, which gave it speed rather than power. BRIAN SHARPE

Below: The predecessors of Gresley's Pacifics were the Atlantics, referring to a 4-4-2 wheel arrangement. GNR No 251 is one of H A Ivatt's later designs, with a much larger boiler than the earlier Atlantics. JEFF COLLEDGE

Why is *Flying Scotsman* a

PACIFIC?

Wheel arrangement	Description	Diagram
0-2-2 eg	Stephenson's *Rocket*	Oo
0-4-0 eg	*Locomotion No 1*	OO
0-4-2 eg	LMR *Lion* or LBSCR *Gladstone*	OOo
4-2-2 eg	GNR Stirling 'Single' No1	ooOo
2-4-0 eg	LNWR No 790 *Hardwicke*	oOO
4-4-0	the classic Victorian passenger engine	ooOO
4-4-2	'Atlantic' as used by the GNR	ooOOo
0-6-0	the classic standard goods engine	OOO
2-6-0	'Mogul'	oOOO
4-6-0	'10-wheeler'	ooOOO
2-6-2	'Prairie'	oOOOo
4-6-2	'Pacific'	ooOOOo
4-6-4	'Hudson'	ooOOOoo
0-8-0		OOOO
0-8-2		OOOOo
2-8-0	'Consolidation'	oOOOO
2-8-2	'Mikado'	oOOOOo
2-8-4	'Berkshire'	oOOOOoo
4-8-2	'Mountain'	ooOOOOo
4-8-4	'Northern'	ooOOOOoo
0-10-0	'Decapod'	OOOOO
2-10-0	eg BR 9F such as *Evening Star*	oOOOOO
2-8-8-2	Garratt, just one example of articulated locomotive designs with separate sets of coupled driving wheels.	oOOOO OOOOo

Flying Scotsman, when built, was the third of 79 LNER Gresley A1/A3 Pacifics. Designed by Gresley, it was built by the London & North Eastern Railway, who classified it as an A1, but why is it called a 'Pacific'?

As steam locomotives grew in size, they were inevitably designed with more wheels, but not all were 'driving' wheels, ie directly powered by the cylinders. In *Rocket*'s case, only the leading wheels are powered, so the wheel arrangement of the engine is described as an 0-2-2. The first digit is the leading (carrying) wheels, the middle one the driving (coupled) wheels, and the third the rear carrying wheels.

The more driving wheels an engine has, the more power it is able to transmit to the track, but there are good reasons for not all of a locomotive's wheels being powered. The rigid wheelbase can be unkind to the track, and there are more expensive bearings to maintain.

Eventually locomotives of a certain wheel arrangement started to acquire nicknames. These clearly originated in North America, and tend to refer to the areas where a particular wheel arrangement found favour.

The 4-4-2 'Atlantic' was built for speed on level track and was popular in the relatively flat states of the Eastern Seaboard. The 4-6-0 had more power but less speed and was useful in the Midwest, but its nickname, the '10-wheeler', never caught on in Britain. The 4-6-2 or 'Pacific' combined speed and power, useful on the West Coast, where hundreds of miles of level track could suddenly end with a ferocious gradient into the Sierra Nevada mountains.

This was nothing to the terrain encountered by lines such as the Great Northern Railroad, and nothing less than a massive 4-8-4 was necessary to shift tonnages across the Rockies. These acquired the name 'Northern' and were of the type that eventually found universal favour across the USA and Canada.

British express steam power consisted mainly of 4-4-0s, 4-4-2s and 4-6-0s, until the coming of the 4-6-2s in the early 1920s. Even the adoption of the transatlantic Atlantic and Pacific names as descriptions of the engine types probably owed a lot to East Coast Main Line (especially Great Northern Railway) marketing spin. Few other railways even had Atlantics, let alone Pacifics, and 'Pacific' had much more public appeal and glamour than 4-6-2 could ever have.

Many of the larger wheel arrangements were rarely used in Britain and, in fact, several, such as 4-6-4, 2-8-2 and even 2-6-2, were seen almost exclusively in Gresley's later designs.

The 'Whyte' system of wheel arrangements was not universal. France referred only to axles, so a 4-6-2 was a 231. Turkey used driving axles and total axles, so a 2-8-0 was a 450. Initially, diesels used the Whyte system, but as powered bogies became the norm, Bo-Bo and Co-Co came in to use; B being a two-axle bogie, and C three-axle, the o denoting both being powered. An A1A-A1A has two three-axle bogies but with the centre one of each unpowered.

Below: No 4472 *Flying Scotsman* is a Pacific; a 4-6-2. The front four-wheel bogie under the cylinders guides the engine smoothly round curves, and helps support the heaviest part of the engine. Six coupled driving wheels can transmit more power to the track than four wheels. Although eight driving wheels would give more power still, this was never successfully used in Britain for express locomotives. As the engines were just too long and rigid for the curves on British main lines, although eight driving wheels became standard for express engines in many other countries such as the USA. The rear two wheels under the cab were not an articulated pony truck on a Gresley Pacific, but a 'Cartazzi' truck, where the frames were rigid right to the rear of the engine, with side-play in the axleboxes to allow for sideways movement on curves. BRIAN SHARPE

The
GROUPING

Above: The LNER and LMSR came into existence on 1 January 1923. The LNER's *Flying Scotsman* stands alongside the LMSR's Stanier Pacific No 6201 *Princess Elizabeth,* the first Pacific design introduced by the competing LMS, but not until as late as 1933.
BRIAN SHARPE

On 1 January 1923, Britain's independent railway companies merged to form what have become known as the Big Four: the Great Western Railway, the Southern Railway, the London Midland & Scottish Railway and the London & North Eastern Railway.

The GWR, in fact, was relatively unchanged, apart from absorbing the various small independent companies in south Wales and the Cambrian Railways.

The Southern Railway was a fairly simple amalgamation of the South Eastern & Chatham Railway, the London Brighton & South Coast Railway and the London & South Western Railway.

The LMSR principally combined the Midland Railway, the London & North Western Railway and, in Scotland, the Caledonian Railway, the Highland Railway and the Glasgow & South Western Railway. The Lancashire & Yorkshire Railway and the North London Railway had already merged into the LNWR,

and the LMSR also took in the North Staffordshire, Furness and Maryport & Carlisle railways.

The LNER was an amalgamation of the Great Northern, Great Central, Great Eastern and North Eastern railways in England, and the North British and Great North of Scotland railways north of the border. The Hull & Barnsley Railway had already merged with the NER, but the Midland & Great Northern Joint Railway was to remain independent until 1936.

The effect of the 'Grouping' on the *Flying Scotsman* story was twofold. The train, the 10am from King's Cross and corresponding up working from Edinburgh, was now run by one company throughout, as was the competing train on the West Coast Main Line. The engine, No 1472, about to be built, and which would shortly become *Flying Scotsman*, although built to run on the Great Northern Railway between King's Cross and York, was now likely to run much farther afield, perhaps to Edinburgh or even beyond.

GNR/LNER
locomotive classes

The engine types of the Great Northern Railway were reclassified by the LNER although, where possible, the same ones were retained, and the other constituent companies' classes altered to fit. The GNR had rightly called its new Pacifics A1s and this was continued. On the LNER, the letter denoted the wheel arrangement. The number within the wheel arrangement was generally in order of the constituent companies. So the GNR Pacifics were A1s and the NER Pacifics A2s. As classes were rendered extinct by withdrawals, their numbers were taken by new LNER designs. As far as possible, the GNR classifications were used, but the opportunity was taken to make the system more logical.

A. **4-6-2 'Pacific':** including original A1 such as *Flying Scotsman*, and A3 rebuilds, NER Raven A2 and later Gresley's streamlined A4. Also GCR and NER 4-6-2 tank engines.

B. **4-6-0:** including Gresley's B17 'Sandringhams', but Thompson's B1 being the most common.

C. **4-4-2:** 'Atlantic', built by most pre-Grouping constituents of the LNER, but mostly withdrawn by early BR days, apart from tank engines.

D. **4-4-0:** including the GER Claud Hamiltons, GCR Directors, and NBR 'Glens', and Gresley's D49 'Hunts & Shires'

E. **2-4-0:** The GER E4s ran well into BR days in the 1950s.

F. **2-4-2:** mostly tank engines

G. **0-4-4:** mostly tank engines

H. **4-4-4:** The NER built a few, as did the Metropolitan Railway

J. **0-6-0:** of numerous varieties, including early diesel shunters.

K. **2-6-0:** Gresley's GNR K2 and K3, and LNER K4, plus Thompson's later K1.

L. **2-6-4:** all were tank engines.

M. **0-6-4:** a few tank engines

N. **0-6-2:** mostly tank engines, including Ivatts N1 and Gresley's N2 for King's Cross suburban trains.

O. **2-8-0:** including the GCR O4, adopted by the WD in the First World War, and Gresley's first three-cylinder design for the GNR.

P. **2-8-2:** The P1s were Gresley's LNER goods engines, but the P2s were his biggest express engines, such as No 2001 *Cock o' the North*.

Q. **0-8-0:** large goods engines, especially on the NER and GNR.

R. **0-8-2:**

S. **0-8-4:**

T. **4-8-0:**

U: The unique Garratt, No 9999, a 2-8-8-2.

V. **2-6-2:** rare in Britain, but Gresley's V2 'Green Arrows' were exceptional.

W. **4-6-4:** again rare, but Gresley built one, the experimental water-tube boilered No 10000. Technically it was, in fact, a 4-6-2-2.

X. **2-2-4 and 4-2-2**

Y. **0-4-0** small tank engines.

Z **0-4-2**
The LNER locomotive classifications continued in use throughout BR days, for ex-LNER engines.

Above: The GNR standard goods engine, the J22 0-6-0 became the J6 in LNER classification. J was retained by the LNER from the GNR as denoting 0-6-0. The numbering for the classification normally ran through GNR, GCR, GER, NER, NBR and GNSR in that order, with LNER-built classes taking later numbers, eg J72 and J94. There were exceptions to this general rule though.
PAUL CHANCELLOR COLLECTION

'The Flying Scotsman'
THE TRAIN

When the LNER decided to name its engine No 1472 for its star appearance at the 1924 Wembley exhibition, the name chosen was *Flying Scotsman*. This was the name unofficially given to the premier Anglo-Scottish express train from King's Cross, the 10am to Edinburgh, a service that dated right back to Great Northern Railway days in 1864.

At that time, the train was the fastest on the East Coast route – allowed, for example, just 1hr 35min to cover 76.4 miles from King's Cross to Peterborough, a time that remained relatively unaltered throughout steam days. Arrival at Edinburgh was at 8.30pm, a time

that also remained unaltered for many years, but gradually reduced as locomotives became more powerful.

The GNR was responsible for operating the train as far as York, and stops were made at Peterborough, Grantham and Retford. For much of its earlier years, the 10 o'clock passed non-stop through Doncaster. In fact, for several years, a slip coach was included, which was detached on the move to serve Doncaster. Another slip coach for a few years was detached at Essendine for Stamford passengers.

By 1910, the train was running from King's Cross as far as York with only one stop, at Grantham, and was reaching Edinburgh in 8hr 45min and, during the summer, a 9.50am relief ran, non-stop to Doncaster,

FLYING SCOTSMAN

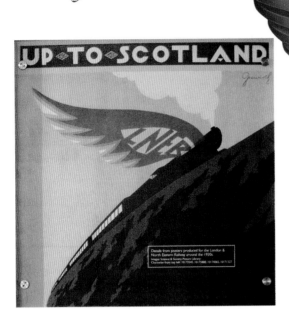

then non-stop to Newcastle with a North Eastern Railway engine.

The train was colloquially known as the 'Special Scotch Express', then 'The Flying Scotchman', said to have originated partly from the famous ship *The Flying Dutchman*, but also as express stage coaches were often referred to as 'Flying'. However, officially, the GNR always referred to the train simply as the 10 o'clock.

The LNER continued running the train and the new Gresley A1 Pacifics were an ideal choice of motive power from 1923. In 1927, the relief train started running non-stop from King's Cross to Newcastle, with A1 Pacific No 4475 *Flying Fox* being the engine chosen to inaugurate what was to be one of the longest regular non-stop workings by a steam engine. By then, the 'Flying Scotchman' had become known as the 'Flying Scotsman' and, from 1927, the train officially became the 'Flying Scotsman', with its title appearing in timetables, on carriage roofboards and on a headboard carried on the engine.

The rival LMS was outdoing the LNER by running non-stop between Euston and Carlisle, using a Royal Scot 4-6-0, and this was slightly farther than King's Cross to Newcastle. The two companies had a gentlemen's agreement not to compete for the fastest speeds on the Anglo-Scottish runs, partly for safety reasons, and competition was in the form of publicity and passenger comfort and amenities.

The LNER on 1 May 1928 started to run their 10am 'Flying Scotsman' service non-stop from King's Cross to Edinburgh and, appropriately enough, the engine that hauled the first northbound train was No 4472 *Flying Scotsman* itself. The launch of this service was a huge media event, and the 'Flying Scotsman' was seen by the sort of crowds that witness the engine's passage today. Times have changed in that the first run of a regular daily service could command such public and media interest.

The LMS actually beat the LNER a few days earlier by running non-stop from Euston to both Glasgow and Edinburgh. However these were one-offs; the LMS could not expect its crews to run that kind of distance daily. The LNER, though, had fitted some of its Pacifics, including *Flying Scotsman*, with corridor tenders so the crews could be changed en route.

The 'Flying Scotsman' continued to run, almost without interruption, as other named trains on the route came and went. It was accelerated in 1932 for the first time in 32 years but, by 1938, the 'Coronation' was faster. From 1949, the 'Capitals Limited' became the Edinburgh non-stop service, renamed the 'Elizabethan' in 1953. Only with the introduction of the Deltic diesels in 1961 was the 'Flying Scotsman' accelerated to equal the pre-war steam times of the 'Coronation'. The 'Elizabethan' was never dieselised and was worked by Gresley A4 Pacifics to the end. Some of the pre-war 'Silver Jubilee' and 'Coronation' streamliners, the post-war 'Capitals Limited' and 'Elizabethan', and the diesel-era 'Silver Jubilee' were faster, some ran non-stop to Edinburgh while the 'Scotsman' started to pause at Newcastle, but they were all short-lived by comparison. The 10am 'Flying Scotsman' survived them all until 1982, when its departure time was changed to 10.35am.

Above: No 4472 *Flying Scotsman* carries the BR-era headboard. BRIAN SHARPE

Above left: The LNER 'Flying Scotsman' headboard as carried after 1927.

In the diesel era, the 'Flying Scotsman' carried the 'winged thistle' headboard, probably the only instance where a train was so famous it did not actually need the name to identify it.

Flying Scotsman
THE ENGINE

By the time Nigel Gresley's third A1 Pacific No 1472 actually took to the rails, the Great Northern Railway had become part of the London & North Eastern Railway when the independent companies were grouped into the 'Big Four'. Gresley could actually have lost his job through this but, although Robinson of the Great Central was the preferred choice as the CME of the new company in view of his experience, he felt ready to retire and instead recommended Gresley for the job.

The whole course of railway history in Britain could have been very different, and it was Gresley's appointment as the LNER's CME that led to production of his Pacifics being continued. Next came No 1473 but, although No 1471 was given the name *Sir Frederick Banbury* by the LNER, No 1473, like No 1472, remained unnamed.

But were Gresley's A1 Pacifics any good?

Well, at the same time as Gresley's engines rolled out of Doncaster, Sir Vincent Raven of the North Eastern Railway was producing engines of a new Pacific design

at Darlington. These were known as A2s on the LNER and the two types were tested against each other, just to prove to Gresley that his design was best and there was nothing he could learn from Darlington. Raven was a respected engineer and his engines were good, but Gresley's were considered better so the Raven design only ever totalled five engines while production of the Gresley ones continued, to eventually total 79 of the A1/A3 class.

When *Flying Scotsman* appeared at the British Empire Exhibition at Wembley in 1924, it stood next to the GWR's 4-6-0 No 4073 *Caerphilly Castle*, which the GWR's publicity described as Britain's most powerful express engine.

Gresley's A1 design was also tested against Collett's GWR Castles on both LNER and GWR routes to try to prove which really was the most powerful. Certainly the Castle was considered to be the pinnacle of locomotive design in Britain, although they were only 4-6-0s and, perhaps surprisingly, the Castle won in this contest, particularly in terms of economy, although even in

Below: A1 Pacific No 1472 *Flying Scotsman*, as prepared for display at the British Empire Exhibition at Wembley in 1924.

What if?

If Gresley had not been appointed Chief Mechanical Engineer of the LNER, Robinson, or possibly someone else, would have been appointed, and the new Pacifics could have had a much less certain future. Even if the new man had not favoured Gresley's more radical design features such as conjugated valve gear, no one could have rebuilt the A1s or come up with an alternative Pacific design in time for the 1924 Wembley Exhibition.

An A1 would almost certainly still have been selected and the name *Flying Scotsman* is likely still to have been carried. *Flying Scotsman*'s initial claim to fame would still have been there and the combination of the most elegant and powerful-looking Pacific and the most inspired choice of name bestowed on a steam engine would still have assured it a place in railway history.

However, it could have been short-lived. A new CME might not have persisted with the design and acted on the results of the comparative trials with the GWR Castle, as did Gresley. The A1 was not actually as good as it looked initially, and a new CME might have simply thought he could do better and come up with his own new design, which would have been selected for the record non-stop runs and speed trials.

Other steam designs elsewhere proved that they could attain speeds of well over 100mph, and it was the limitations of the routes they ran on, rather than any design weakness, that prevented them from achieving *Mallard*'s 126mph record.

Another designer's engine might well have attained the steam speed record for the LNER, and *Flying Scotsman*'s fame would then have been brief. It might even have remained one of a handful of engines, like Raven's LNER A2 Pacifics, to be scrapped in the 1930s. Perhaps the name would have been reused and *Flying Scotsman* might still have gone on to become the most famous steam engine in the world, albeit a completely different engine.

All this is not just conjecture, but unlikely. Sir Nigel Gresley was one of the greatest engineers ever to have lived and his achievements were already so prolific by 1922 that his appointment as CME by the LNER was virtually assured.

If Robinson had been preferred initially, it could only have been a matter of time before Gresley succeeded him. Unless he had left and joined another railway…

power output the Castle had the slight edge, so there was obviously still room for improvement in the LNER design.

The two designs had been produced for very different routes and to use very different types of coal, so they were difficult to compare.

Gresley took the lessons on board, in particular the use of long-lap piston valves. This, together with increasing the boiler pressure from 180 to 220psi, increasing the amount of superheating, and slightly reducing cylinder diameter, transformed the A1s.

The new engines incorporating the design changes were called 'super-Pacifics' and classified A3. Later engines were built as A3s and, eventually, all but one of the A1s were to be rebuilt to A3 specification.

However, despite the *Castle*'s superiority in the

contest, the name was just never going to stick in people's minds quite like *Flying Scotsman*.

Flying Scotsman had the name that made it a natural choice for any publicity-oriented stunt the LNER wanted to stage, so it quite naturally took part in the 1929 publicity film *Flying Scotsman* but did not haul the inaugural non-stop train to Newcastle in 1927. It did, though, haul the rather more important first non-stop to Edinburgh on 1 May the following year.

It was also one of the engines chosen to take part in some high-speed test running in 1934, in the course of which it not only broke the 100mph barrier but did it while hauling a train carrying scientific equipment to record its speed. It may not really have been the first steam locomotive to reach 100mph, but it was definitely the first one officially and scientifically recorded as having done so. The name *Flying Scotsman* on the engine just always seemed to attract rather more media coverage for these exploits than might have been the case with any other engine.

It was No 2750 *Papyrus* that hit 108mph soon afterwards, but how many people have ever heard of it?

Above: The 'Caledonian' was introduced by BR in 1957, running between Euston and Glasgow, initially hauled by Stanier's Duchess Pacifics, but the impressive headboard continued in use into the diesel era.

Below: The locomotive used on the Southern Railway's 'Golden Arrow' was the most highly decorated ever to run in daily service in Britain, with a full smokebox headboard, British and French flags on the bufferbeam, and even a huge golden arrow on the side of the locomotive.

THE STORY

of named trains in Britain

Important express trains have been named since the early days of long-distance train travel, following the traditions of the days of stage coaches but, in most cases, initially the name was not officially given to the train by the railway that ran it.

Britain is actually behind other countries in naming its trains, but this is partly because of the sheer volume of trains that run in this country. In the United States, most lines see only one passenger train per day, so naturally it is named.

Today, many of the famous named trains, as opposed to locomotives, are well-known to most people, although in most cases, in the era of standardisation and modern traction, the names are rarely now used.

It is sometimes difficult to establish exactly when a train received its name; certainly it is very rare to see photographs of pre-Grouping trains with headboards carried on the locomotive. In many cases, the train name seems to have been used mainly in advertising and publicity, especially for summer holiday trains. A classic example is the 'Irish Mail', a title used right from the first train from Euston to Holyhead connecting with the boat to Ireland in 1848, but not distinguished officially even by carriage roofboards until 1927.

The Great Eastern Railway half-heartedly named one train in 1897 the 'Cromer Express' and, when it changed it in 1907 to the 'Norfolk Coast Express', did provide it with carriage roofboards but no locomotive headboard.

The names used in the early part of the 20th century reflect the era when language was different to today. One of the first named trains to run in Britain appears to have been the 'Brighton Sunday Pullman Limited', from around 1899. In 1908 it became the slightly more modern-sounding 'Southern Belle' and the 'Brighton Belle' from soon after electrification in 1932.

At the other end of Britain, Scottish expresses to Aberdeen had been named from 1906, including the Caledonian Railway's 'Granite City' and 'Grampian'. North British Railway locomotives normally carried a destination board on the front of the engine on most passenger services, so this company tended to be at the forefront of the tradition of also identifying its named trains with a locomotive headboard, including the 'Fife Coast Express' from 1910 and the 'Lothian Coast Express' from 1912.

The GER and NBR named trains were early casualties

1 THE IRISH MAIL

2 THE CAPITALS LIMITED

3 THE INTER-CITY

4 THE ELIZABETHAN

of the First World War, but the NBR trains were quickly revived afterwards so the LNER did inherit some named trains, and no doubt the NBR policy was to influence the LNER's decision to name its premier long-distance expresses soon after Grouping in 1923.

The Great Western Railway was certainly a world leader in the early 1900s and its 10.10am Paddington-to-Penzance express ran non-stop to Plymouth from 1904, easily the longest non-stop run at that time. By 1906 it was known as the 'Cornish Riviera Limited', a train which has continued to run almost uninterrupted, apart from a slight change to 'Cornish Riviera Express'. The word 'Limited' in a train name is typical railway parlance and refers to the fact that the train was booked to make only a limited number of stops. These names were hardly compatible with modern marketing-speak.

Another early named train was the 'Sunny South Special', later 'Express', initially a joint London & North Western and London Brighton & South Coast Railway operation, but later extended to a series of Midlands and North, to South Coast summer holiday trains. It is doubtful whether any was ever distinguished with a headboard or carriage roofboards, though.

From 1923, the GWR's 'Cheltenham Spa Express' officially became Britain's fastest train and became known as the 'Cheltenham Flyer', which officially it never was. Again the public knew the name it wanted, but the railway was too staid to listen to public opinion.

Certainly a very early British train to have acquired a name was the 10am King's Cross-to-Edinburgh, referred to as the 'Special Scotch Express' in timetables from 1864 but, from the 1880s, referred to by the public as the 'Flying Scotchman' and later still 'Flying Scotsman'. It was the public that named it, though, not the railway operating authorities, until 1924. It was in 1926-1927 that the LNER recognised there was much to be gained by listening to public opinion, and it not only officially recognised the name 'Flying Scotsman', already by then carried on A1 Pacific No 4472, but, at the same time, the 'Aberdonian', 'Night Scotsman' and 'Scarborough Flyer' names were given official recognition, followed by the 'Queen of Scots' Pullman in 1928.

The railway publicity machines started working to good effect in 1927, and the name 'Flying Scotsman' was simply the best of a great selection of train names that were either updated, officially adopted or dreamed up at around this time.

The LNER was not unique and not necessarily the trendsetter. At the same time, the Southern Railway's 'Atlantic Coast Express' was named, as was the GWR's 'Cambrian Coast Express' and the Manchester-to-Bournemouth 'Pines Express'.

The LMSR naturally countered the LNER publicity machine with its 'Royal Scot' and 'Royal Highlander' Anglo-Scottish expresses, yet the carrying of headboards on engines never became standard practice on the LMSR.

On the Southern Railway, the international express from Victoria to Dover became the 'Golden Arrow' in 1929, with its French counterpart carrying the 'Flèche d'Or' insignia. The 'Bournemouth Belle' Pullman followed in 1931.

Surprisingly, the GWR's 'Bristolian' did not come into being until 1935, at around the time the real publicity and speed competition started, with the LNER's 'Silver Jubilee' and 'Coronation' being countered by the LMS 'Coronation Scot'.

During the Second World War, though, only four trains retained their names – the East Coast Main Line's 'Flying Scotsman', 'Night Scotsman' and 'Aberdonian', and the Great Western's 'Cornish Riviera Express'.

It was some time after the war and nationalisation that names were restored, and many of the pre-war names simply disappeared.

The 'Capitals Limited' was an uninspiring choice of name for a new King's Cross-to-Edinburgh non-stop in 1949, although calling it the 'Elizabethan' from 1953 was better. Other new names also stood the test of time better, even if the trains did not, the East Coast's 'Talisman' and West Coast's 'Caledonian', introduced in 1957, being two of the best-remembered trains of the steam age.

Train naming in Britain is now rather half-hearted, but this simply reflects the consistent standard of speed and service interval now being achieved, with no one train on a route standing apart from the others. In recent times, high-speed trains have even had the train name simply pasted on the front. In such circumstances, it is perhaps better to just abandon the name altogether, but no wonder the British public still hankers after real engines with real names hauling real trains distinguished by a cast metal plate pronouncing itself the 'Flying Scotsman'.

Top: The carriage roofboard came into use some time before locomotive headboards, probably for good reason, as this was what the passengers were more likely to see.

Above 1: The 'Irish Mail' is regarded as Britain's first named train, but this, in fact, related to more than one service, and was not distinguished by a headboard until BR days.

Above 2: The 'Capitals Limited' was introduced by BR in 1949, running non-stop from King's Cross to Edinburgh, but never struck the same chord with the public as 'Flying Scotsman'.

Above 3: 'Inter-City' was a BR innovation, but does date back to 1951, when it was given to a Paddington-to-Birmingham-and-Birkenhead express.

Above 4: The 'Elizabethan' was given to the Edinburgh non-stop in 1953 to commemorate Queen Elizabeth II's coronation, replacing the 'Capitals Limited'.

What's in a
NAME?

T he LNER constituent companies were generally not known for naming their engines. The Great Northern, Great Eastern and North Eastern Railways each had only one or two named engines, while the Great Central and the Great North of Scotland Railways had more 'namers' but not by any means all of their express engines.

Only the North British Railway bestowed names on all of its passenger engines, and they were mostly names inspired by the romantic and beautiful country the line ran through, such as glens, Scottish castles or characters from Sir Walter Scott's novels. Even some goods engines carried names, to commemorate their exploits in the Continent during the First World War. The NBR, though, never gave its engines cast nameplates; they remained painted on, right through LNER and BR days.

While Gresley of the Great Northern became Chief Mechanical Engineer of the LNER, the first chairman of the new company was William Whitelaw, a North British man, and he appears to have influenced the new company's decision to start naming its locomotives. First came the five NER Raven A2 Pacifics, given city names connected with the area they worked in. The GNR A1s, likely to be far more numerous, would soon have exhausted this theme, and somehow St Neots, Grimsby and Biggleswade may not have had quite the right ring to them. *Sir Frederick Banbury*, the last chairman of the GNR, was commemorated on No 1471, and for the British Empire Exhibition at Wembley in 1924, No 1472 became *Flying Scotsman*.

Although it is believed there was never an actual racehorse called *Flying Scotsman*, this seems to have been the inspiration behind the decision to name the rest of the class after racehorses and, when naming started in earnest, No 4475 duly acquired the name *Flying Fox*. This was a real public relations masterpiece as it started the LNER's long-running policy of naming its engines after racehorses.

A more appropriate and inspired public relations gimmick could hardly have been dreamed of. By choosing the names of the winners of the classic races, many of them winners of the St Leger, run at Doncaster, it cemented the relationship between the railway and horseracing industries of Doncaster, and helped some of the LNER's express engines to become household names.

It should not be forgotten that the clientele who used the long-distance express trains in the 1920s and 1930s were very much the riding and shooting classes, and the racehorse names would strike a chord with many of the passengers.

Naming individual steam engines is not exclusively a British tradition, but it has never been as widespread in other countries. Early American engines were frequently named, but few European engines ever carried names of any description. Some Asian and African countries also bestowed names on engines in the early days of their railways, but only Britain continued to name virtually all of its passenger engines right up to the end of steam and beyond. This had been inconsistent up to 1923, but once the LNER joined the other three Big Four companies, it was to become accepted practice for very many years.

City of Newcastle **was the name given to the first North Eastern Railway A2 Pacific. The plate is smaller than those on the A1s, but of a higher standard of finish, Darlington having more experience of casting plates as NER engines did carry numberplates, even if they were all previously unnamed.**
BRIAN SHARPE

Locomotive-naming policy of Britain's railways Pre-1923

Great Western Railway: All passenger engines named: eg. cities, stars, earls, saints.
South Eastern & Chatham Railway: Engines unnamed in later years.
London Brighton & South Coast Railway: All passenger engines carried painted names, often towns served by the railway.
London & South Western Railway: Most engines unnamed.
Great Eastern Railway: Only one engine named.
Great Northern Railway: Only one engine named before No 1470 *Great Northern* in 1922.
Great Central Railway: Many engines named; directors, military etc.
Midland Railway: Engines unnamed.
London & North Western Railway: Passenger engines named; patriotic, military, royalty, mythology, astronomy etc.
Cambrian Railways: Engines unnamed.
North Staffordshire Railway: Engines unnamed.
Furness Railway: Engines unnamed.
Lancashire & Yorkshire Railway: Engines unnamed.
North Eastern Railway: Only one engine named.
North British Railway: All passenger engines named; Sir Walter Scott novels, glens etc.
Caledonian Railway. Many engines named; usually Scottish, including directors' houses.
Glasgow & South Western Railway: Engines unnamed.
Highland Railway: Passenger engines named; usually Scottish eg lochs, bens.
Great North of Scotland Railway: A few engines named; Various, including military.

Post-Grouping, virtually all new passenger engines carried names

Great Western Railway: castles, kings, halls, manors, granges, counties.
Southern Railway: King Arthur legends, schools, military and maritime, West Country places, shipping lines.
London Midland & Scottish Railway: military, royalty, Commonwealth, legendary figures, cities.
London & North Eastern Railway: racehorses, directors, birds, Commonwealth, stately homes, foxhunts, football teams, antelopes.

British Railways (steam)

Famous Britons, Scottish themes, firths, clans

It was the LNER who were ahead of the game here. While the other companies continued the military and patriotic traditions inherited from their constituent companies, the LNER went first for racehorses, then fast-flying birds and antelopes, and even football teams. Many of these names aroused more public interest, were often associated with speed and lent themselves sometimes to elaborate naming ceremonies.

This was to set the scene for many years later when BR started to name diesel locomotives after city councils, corporate customers or TV programmes, where they could exploit every last bit of local publicity from a naming ceremony, the name often only being carried on a temporary basis.

Doncaster Works had little experience of casting nameplates, having only ever produced the two tiny 'Henry' and 'Oakley' plates for the pioneer Atlantic No 990. The A1 Pacific plates not only had a very rough finish by comparison with those on other railways, but they were too thin, and tended to crack. Even *Flying Scotsman* lost its name at one point when the plate cracked in two.

New, thicker plates were designed, with large mounting brackets. These are now unpopular with collectors as they are difficult to mount flush on a wall. The curved A1-style nameplates that were carried over the centre driving wheel splashers were all of a standard size, regardless of the number of letters in the name.

A few of the A1 Pacifics were not named after racehorses. These included the first three, *Great Northern, Sir Frederick Banbury, Flying Scotsman, Centenary,* which commemorated the Stockton & Darlington anniversary, and *Prince of Wales,* which happened to be under repair when the then Prince of Wales visited Doncaster Works. another was originally named *William Whitelaw,* but the plate was transferred to a new A4 class Pacific. *Dick Turpin* and *Knight of the Thistle* were also not racehorses although, surprisingly, *Doncaster* and *Diamond Jubilee* were.
BRIAN SHARPE

The A1s and A3s

A1				BR number
1470	4470	Great Northern	Rebuilt as Thompson prototype A1 1945	60113
1471	4471	Sir Frederick Banbury	A3 from 1942	60102
1472	4472	Flying Scotsman	A10 from 1945: A3 from 1947	60103
1473	4473	Solario	A3 from 1941	60104
1474	4474	Victor Wild	A3 from 1942	60105
1475	4475	Flying Fox	A10 from 1945: A3 from 1947	60106
1476	4476	Royal Lancer	A10 from 1945: A3 from 1946	60107
1477	4477	Gay Crusader	A3 from 1943	60108
1478	4478	Hermit	A3 from 1943	60109
1479	4479	Robert The Devil	A3 from 1942	60110
1480N	4480	Enterprise	A3 from 1927	60111
1481N	4481	St Simon	A10 from 1945: A3 from 1946	60112
2543		Melton	A10 from 1945: A3 from 1947	60044
2544		Lemberg	A3 from 1927	60045
2545		Diamond Jubilee	A3 from 1941	60046
2546		Donovan	A10 from 1945: A3 from 1947	60047
2547		Doncaster	A10 from 1945: A3 from 1946	60048
2548		Galtee More	A10 then A3 from 1945	60049
2549		Persimmon	A3 from 1943	60050
2555		Blink Bonny	A10 then A3 from 1945	60051
2551		Prince Palatine	A3 from 1941	60052
2552		Sansovino	A3 from 1943	60053
2553		Prince of Wales	A3 from 1943 (previously Manna)	60054
2554		Woolwinder	A3 from 1942	60055
2555		Centenary	A3 from 1944	60056
2556		Ormonde	A10 from 1945: A3 from 1947	60057
2557		Blair Athol	A10 then A3 from 1945	60058
2558		Tracery	A3 from 1942	60059
2559		The Tetrarch	A3 from 1942	60060
2560		Pretty Polly	A3 from 1944	60061
2561		Minoru	A3 from 1944	60062
2562		Isinglass	A10 from 1945: A3 from 1946	60063
2563		Tagalie	A3 from 1942 (William Whitelaw)	60064
2564		Knight of Thistle	A10 from 1945: A3 from 1947	60065
2565		Merry Hampton	A10 then A3 from 1945	60066
2566		Ladas	A3 from 1939	60067
2567		Sir Visto	A10 from 1945: A3 from 1948	60068
2568		Sceptre	A3 from 1942	60069
2569		Gladiateur	A10 from 1945: A3 from 1947	60070
2570		Tranquil	A3 from 1944	60071

2571	*Sunstar*	A3 from 1941	60072
2572	*St Gatien*	A10 then A3 from 1945	60073
2573	*Harvester*	A3 from 1928	60074
2574	*St Frusquin*	A3 from 1942	60075
2575	*Galopin*	A3 from 1941	60076
2576	*The White Knight*	A3 from 1943	60077
2577	*Night Hawk*	A3 from 1944	60078
2578	*Bayardo*	A3 from 1928	60079
2579	*Dick Turpin*	A3 from 1942	60080
2580	*Shotover*	A3 from 1928	60081
2581	*Neil Gow*	A3 from 1943	60082
2582	*Sir Hugo*	A3 from 1941	60083

Engines built as A3 from 1928

2743	*Felstead*	60089
2744	*Grand Parade*	60090
2745	*Captain Cuttle*	60091
2746	*Fairway*	60092
2747	*Coronach*	60093
2748	*Colorado*	60094
2749	*Flamingo*	60095
2750	*Papyrus*	60096
2751	*Humorist*	60097
2752	*Spion Kop*	60098
2595	*Trigo*	60084
2596	*Manna*	60085
2597	*Gainsborough*	60086
2795	*Call Boy*	60099
2796	*Spearmint*	60100
2797	*Cicero*	60101
2598	*Blenheim*	60087
2599	*Book Law*	60088
2500	*Windsor Lad*	60035
2501	*Colombo*	60036
2502	*Hyperion*	60037
2503	*Firdaussi*	60038
2504	*Sandwich*	60039
2505	*Cameronian*	60040
2506	*Salmon Trout*	60041
2507	*Singapore*	60042
2508	*Brown Jack*	60043

The engines are shown in chronological order of construction, from 1922 to 1935. The LNER numbering system was confusing and, when engines were renumbered, they were not kept in their original order at all, so the eventual BR numbering of the class is really quite haphazard, with the original engines carrying the highest numbers.

Not all of the engines were built at Doncaster, Nos 2563 to 2582 being built by the North British Locomotive Company in Glasgow.

THE TON

to accomplish the journey non-stop.

In fact the fastest train in Britain in the early 1930s was the GWR 'Cheltenham Spa Express', known unofficially as the 'Cheltenham Flyer', on which the Castle class 4-6-0 was booked to average 71.3mph between Swindon and Paddington. The GWR was never a railway to push for maximum top speeds, though, and had never really publicised the fact that 4-4-0 No 3440 *City of Truro* had allegedly hit 102.3mph in 1904.

Gresley intended to introduce a new, long distance, high-speed train service in 1935 and conducted some tests with A1 and A3 Pacifics, during which first *Flying Scotsman* reached 100mph, then *Papyrus* 108mph.

On 30 November 1934, with renowned driver William Sparshatt in charge, A1 No 4472 took four coaches 185.8 miles from King's Cross to Leeds in 151 minutes six seconds. Another two coaches were added and, between Little Bytham and Essendine, in Lincolnshire, No 4472 is claimed to have broken the 100mph barrier.

In March 1935

the appearance that was radically different – the streamlined casing, inspired by the shape of a Bugatti racing car and perfected in wind-tunnel tests, set off by a silver colour scheme, making the A4 the most striking steam engine ever seen. It is actually questionable whether streamlining made the engines any faster, but it certainly aroused huge media interest.

The engines were designed to work the 'Silver Jubilee' the 232.3 miles from Darlington to King's Cross at an average of 70.4mph, only slightly slower than the GWR train but over more than twice the distance. On the Press demonstration run of 27 September 1935, the brand-new Gresley A4 No 2509 *Silver Link* twice hit 112mph, taking the world record away from the A3 *Papyrus*. This made *Silver Link* a household name at the time, but its fame has not endured to anything like the extent of *Flying Scotsman*.

When the second streamlined train, the 'Coronation' was introduced, it brought the King's Cross-to-Edinburgh time d

similar to the A3 but with a higher boiler pressure, at 250psi, and slightly reduced cylinder diameter, to give greater power. It was

Gresley still wanted to hold the record, though, and arranged some braking tests, on which the engine to be used was the fairly new but well run-in double-

ABOVE: Two Gresley record-breakers together: 126mph A4 streamlined Pacific No 4468 *Mallard* and first authenticated 100mph A3 Pacific No 4472 *Flying Scotsman* run light engine towards Hatton on the GWR main line on 26 October 1986. Both engines had hauled separate trains from Marylebone to Banbury, and travelled together to turn before heading their respective trains back from Stratford-upon-Avon. BRIAN SHARPE

chimneyed A4 No 4468 *Mallard*. Although the tests were to be conducted south of Peterborough, Gresley asked for the train to go north to Barkston Junction, to return down Stoke Bank, the line's fastest stretch of track. The officials on board were told at Grantham they would be trying for the record and were given the option of disembarking. None did, and No 4468 topped 126mph, setting the world steam speed record that has never been bettered.

By then the LNER's naming policy had moved on and, although *Mallard* and *Silver Link* both became household names in the 1930s, *Silver Link* was probably the second best-known engine after *Flying Scotsman*, by virtue of its silver livery and dramatic public debut rather than by its name. The A4 names just did not capture the public's imagination quite like the racehorses, *Flying Scotsman* especially.

The outbreak of war stopped any further record attempts, and it was well into the BR era before speeds returned to anything like their pre-war levels. It is a Gresley A4 Pacific, No 60007 *Sir Nigel Gresley*, which holds the post-war British steam speed record – 112mph – set on Stoke Bank in 1959.

In later BR steam days, 100mph-plus speeds were relatively commonplace, although rarely authenticated. Some of Gresley's A4s, now 30 years old, were still achieving the ton on the Glasgow-to-Aberdeen three-hour expresses in the mid-1960s and, in particular, several Southern Railway Bulleid Pacifics are said to have achieved speeds of well over 100mph in their last few days of service on the Bournemouth main line in 1967.

We are a little parochial in Britain, though, and we forget that many other countries built some superb express steam engines which, in most cases, had much longer, straighter, faster stretches of track to run on. Many American engines are claimed to have exceeded 100mph and, although there is insufficient definite proof, it is highly likely that Philadelphia & Reading Railroad 'Camelback' Atlantic No 343 reached 100mph on 14 June 1907, and Pennsylvania Railroad E6 Atlantic No 460 did likewise on 11 June 1927. The fastest were the Milwaukee Road 4-6-4s, of which No 6402 on 20 July 1934 in tests for the introduction of the high-speed 'Hiawatha' service between Chicago and Milwaukee, averaged 90mph for 69 miles, undoubtedly exceeding 100mph in the process.

The 'Hiawatha' in regular service was actually scheduled to average 100mph, and it is known that one held the world speed record prior to *Mallard*.

No doubt many French and German engines could also claim the unofficial record, but the only scientifically-validated feat was 124.5mph by a streamlined Bavarian Pacific in 1935. This engine actually achieved this speed on two separate occasions and on an undulating section of track, whereas *Mallard*'s 126mph was all downhill. Scientific evidence of the German engine's feats exist but are incomplete. It is highly likely that it may have just touched a higher maximum than *Mallard* but, with the Second World War looming, the rest of the world was not really interested in German claims to world records at the time.

Again the LNER's marketing 'spin' seems to have worked: *Flying Scotsman* is believed by many to have been the first 100mph locomotive and Gresley's *Mallard* has come to be regarded as the fastest steam engine in the world.

FLYING SCOTSM

LNER
Pacific classifications

Gresley's Great Northern Railway Pacifics were referred to as the A1 class by the GNR and subsequently the LNER and, logically, the five Pacifics built by Sir Vincent Raven for the North Eastern Railway were referred to as the A2 class. When the A1 design was upgraded, the new engines took the classification A3 as they were quite different, despite the external similarity. Next on the scene were Gresley's streamlined Pacifics in 1935 and these took the

classification A4. So far it was all quite logical.

However, as new A3s were being built, older A1s were being rebuilt to A3 specification so, as they were reclassified, the A1 class was expected to be phased out. By now the classification A5 had been allocated to the Pacific tank engines inherited from the Great Central Railway, with other 4-6-2Ts taking other A-class numbers.

When Gresley died in office in 1941 and Edward Thompson took over as the LNER's Chief Mechanical Engineer, he introduced some new designs, but Gresley designs continued to be built.

Thompson disagreed with many of Gresley's design principles. He took Gresley's P2 2-8-2s and rebuilt them as Pacifics in 1943, calling them A2s, as by 1937 the five NER-built A2 Pacifics had been withdrawn and scrapped, so the classification A2 was spare. The LNER was still turning out Gresley's V2 class of 2-6-2, which had acquitted themselves brilliantly in wartime service, their smaller wheels giving them the power to move prodigious tonnages. Thompson had the last four completed as Pacifics in 1944 and also called them A2s although, apart from the size of their driving wheels, there was little discernible similarity between the two new designs of A2. Gresley had been a firm believer in standardisation of parts, so A1/A3s and A4s had identical 6ft 8in diameter driving wheels, while V2s and P2s had identical 6ft 2in diameter driving wheels.

Although complicated enough, this is by no means the end of the story of the LNER Pacific classes, as Thompson felt he could even improve on Gresley's Pacific design. He went further than just building a new one; he actually rebuilt Gresley's original masterpiece, none other than the pioneer A1, No 4470 *Great Northern*, as his prototype. Rightly or wrongly, it was felt that the new design should be called the A1 despite the fact that there were still many of the original A1s still running. Wartime had held up the rebuilding programme and delayed production of Thompson's 'new' Pacific until the end of the war. However, in April 1945, the last unrebuilt A1s which, perhaps surprisingly, included *Flying Scotsman*, were reclassified A10.

Thompson's A1 still had three cylinders, albeit with three separate sets of valve gear, and there were some external design similarities to Gresley's non-streamlined Pacifics, but it was a more functional, less complicated design built for power and ease of maintenance, not speed and elegance. *Great Northern* kept its name, though, and further engines in the class mostly continued the tradition of being named after racehorses.

One of Thompson's design principles, which he did not share with Gresley, was that all connecting rods, ie those from the pistons to the driving wheels, should be of equal length; Gresley was happy to vary the length provided they all drove on the same axle. Thompson's three-cylinder Pacifics therefore looked ungainly, with the outside cylinders set well back to drive the middle axle, while the inside cylinder was well forward between the frames but drove the leading axle using the same length connecting rod as outside.

It was perhaps fortunate that the war ended and Thompson could build new engines, or the remaining 17 original A1s could easily have been rebuilt to Thompson A1 design, and the original *Flying Scotsman* could have disappeared in the 1940s. As it was, the pre-war rebuilding programme was resumed, with No 4472 finally becoming an A3 in 1947 and the last one, No 60068 *Sir Visto*, in BR days in 1949.

It was left to AH Peppercorn, who briefly succeeded

Thompson just before nationalization, to build some new A2 Pacifics, to a slightly more conventional external style, and the various Pacifics with 6ft 2in driving wheels were known as A2s, A2/1s, A2/2s and A2/3s. Peppercorn also started building the rest of the A1 class started by Thompson, but most of the Peppercorn A1 and A2 Pacific classes were actually built by British Railways after nationalisation.

They were good, strong, reliable and, above all, economical engines; they just lacked something of the style of *Flying Scotsman* and the Gresley Pacifics. But they were built in totally different circumstances and, in post-war operating conditions, the various LNER Pacifics all ran very successfully side-by-side.

All of Peppercorn's A1s were scrapped by 1966, but the last working A2, No 60532 *Blue Peter*, was purchased by the late Geoff Drury in 1969 and has seen main line action in recent years. The A1 Trust is, however constructing a brand-new A1, to be known as No 60163 *Tornado*. It will make a fascinating comparison with *Flying Scotsman* when it is completed in just a few years' time.

Above: Pioneer Gresley A1 Pacific No 4470 *Great Northern* in LNER days in January 1939, passing Marshmoor.
COLOUR-RAIL

Left: One of the later batch of Peppercorn A2 Pacifics, introduced in 1947, No 60532 *Blue Peter*. The A1s and A2s were externally similar apart from their driving wheel diameters. Gone are the external design touches, such as the smooth-flowing footplate and wheel splashers from the Gresley era. The whole design is more functional and angular. Smoke deflectors were fitted to all new A1s and A2s.
BRIAN SHARPE

THE WAR

The Second World War, of course, put a stop to speed exploits, but there was no rest for Gresley's Pacifics, including *Flying Scotsman*. In March 1939, the engine was transferred from King's Cross shed back to its original home depot of Doncaster and, as late as 1943, it received a coat of all-over wartime black paint.

Express train haulage was at an end for the duration but, like all steam engines during the war, No 4472 was set to work hauling heavy troop trains and even munitions and coal trains, and not necessarily on its normal operating routes. Railway operating in the war years is not particularly well-documented, but there were certainly instances when the most unlikely engines found their way to the opposite end of the country from where they were normally to be seen.

In *Flying Scotsman*'s case, it changed depots in 1944 more times than most LNER Pacifics did in their entire working lives, moving first from Doncaster to New England at Peterborough, then over to the one-time Great Central shed at Gorton, in Manchester, briefly back to King's Cross, but then New England again, and back to Doncaster.

Sir Nigel Gresley died in office in 1941, and was succeeded by Edward Thompson, a man with a very different engineering background, who later achieved some notoriety by completely rebuilding Gresley's pioneer A1 Pacific No 4470 *Great Northern*.

Thompson did not just rebuild engines and totally undermine all of Sir Nigel Gresley's design principles, like building steel coaches instead of teak ones. There were issues that needed addressing, and one was the chaos which the LNER's locomotive numbers had been allowed to descend into. It had made sense when the various independent companies had been combined in 1923 and the LNER had found itself with many engines that duplicated each other's numbers, but then new engines had been given numbers just to fill gaps in the sequence and, by 1946, a new approach was required. The original system had not really taken account of the huge numbers of engines Gresley was going to build. Thompson had two attempts to make order out of chaos and, as a result, on 20 January 1946, No 4472 *Flying Scotsman* became No 502, but by 5 May it had changed again, to No 103.

It was just a short time later, on 18 November 1946, that *Flying Scotsman* entered Doncaster Works for rebuilding to A3 specification. On 4 January 1947 No 103 returned to service in post-war Thompson apple green livery. This was little different to pre-war style except that the ornate shaded gold-leaf lettering was replaced by a slightly more austere plain yellow, with a slight reduction in lining-out, for example on the back of tenders.

ROBIN JONES

BRITISH RAILWAYS

The Second World War took its toll on Britain's railway system. Some companies, particularly the LNER, were in financial difficulties throughout their existence, and the decision was soon taken by the post-war Labour Government to nationalise the railway system.

The much-loved British Railways came into being on 1 January 1948.

It must have been an incredible upheaval for everyone concerned but, for the railway enthusiasts at the time, it was a fascinating few years. BR, of course, inherited thousands of steam engines, many of which should have been withdrawn years earlier, and many of which carried the same number as at least two other engines.

There were far bigger priorities at the time, but steam enthusiasts are interested in the exchange trials, the new numbering system and the new liveries.

BR was organised into six regions. The Eastern Region was made up of the former GNR, GCR and GER routes of the LNER.

The North Eastern Region comprised the ex-NER routes, and the Scottish Region combined all LMS and LNER routes north of the border.

Flying Scotsman was an Eastern Region engine, and acquired the prefix E to its number for a while in March 1948, though retaining LNER apple green livery, but with 'BRITISH RAILWAYS' painted on its tender.

To make decisions on future locomotive policy, engines from the Big Four companies were tested against each other on each other's routes. This did not involve *Flying Scotsman* but, interestingly, it did involve *Mallard*.

The Eastern Region chose Gresley A4s, rather than the newer Thompson A1 Pacific, to prove the superiority of the engines it had inherited. *Mallard* and the other A4s proved strong, fast and economical, but not reliable, as the middle big-ends played up more than once on test.

As Robert Riddles, an LMS man from Crewe, was appointed BR's first Chief Mechanical Engineer, LMS design policy inevitably took the lead after 1948, and three-cylinder designs, with conjugated valve gear, were not going to be the way forward.

BR wanted to establish a corporate identity totally different to its predecessors and, after some experiments, including some particularly lurid colours, settled on blue for express engines, LNWR-style lined black for mixed traffic engines and plain black for goods engines. GWR Brunswick green was adopted for passenger engines but, in practice, not many classes acquired this livery at first. No E103 *Flying Scotsman* was rightly nominated for express blue and emerged in this colour on 16 December 1949, with black and white lining, cream numbers and, for the first time, a smokebox numberplate, a tradition adopted from the LMS.

By now a numbering system had been devised and 60,000 was added to all ex-LNER engine numbers, so *Flying Scotsman* was now No 60103. A badge was designed for the tenders, often referred to as the cycling lion, and this replaced the words British Railways. Perhaps the major cosmetic difference, apart from the colour, was that the wheels and frames were black and unlined.

When built, Gresley's A1s were considered almost too heavy even for the Great Northern main line, and some modifications had taken place before they could venture to Scotland.

With new A1 and A2 Pacifics being built after the war, and considerable numbers of the smaller V2 2-6-2s now available, the LNER, and later BR, gave thought as to whether Pacifics could be used to accelerate services on other lines. The Great Central route from Marylebone to Sheffield and Manchester had already seen Pacifics; the Great Eastern main line from Liverpool Street to Norwich, still worked by underpowered 4-6-0s, was another possibility.

The GCR having been built late, and to a generous loading gauge with Channel Tunnel freight traffic in mind, presented no great problem and, on 4 June 1950, No 60103 *Flying Scotsman*, was transferred back to the GC line, allocated to Leicester shed. It worked not only over the main line out of Marylebone, but sometimes over the Woodhead route across the Pennines between Sheffield and Manchester.

The use of A3s (and V2 2-6-2s) on the Great Central was to last only until a major regional reorganisation in 1958, when the line became part of the London Midland Region. For the first time, a boundary could be drawn between the regions, instead of the following the pre-nationalisation pattern, with considerable overlapping of routes.

In fact, as the railway system returned to normal, A3s found themselves able to venture to other parts of the system, where they had previously been considered too heavy, but the Eastern Region remained nervous of allowing them into East Anglia, where they could have accelerated services considerably.

It was during its brief fling on the GCR that *Flying Scotsman* lost its BR blue livery. It was found that the colour could not be touched up after repairs, and a total repaint was necessary each time.

On 14 March 1952, No 60103 emerged from works in Brunswick green, which it was to carry for the rest of its BR career. Although basically a Great Western livery, the black and orange lining was in a different style from the GWR. The tender badge and cream numbers were retained and, in common with normal Doncaster practice in BR days, the cylinder covers were unlined black.

On 15 November 1953, *Flying Scotsman* returned to GN main line but was allocated to Grantham, which was the normal engine-changing point for East Coast Main Line expresses.

On 7 April, though, *Flying Scotsman* found itself back at 'Top Shed', reallocated to King's Cross (34A). LNER engines traditionally spent long periods allocated to one shed, and some were never reallocated in their entire lives, so *Flying Scotsman* was actually relatively well-travelled.

It was not until well after the end of the war, and nationalisation in 1948, that the LNER Pacifics returned to their former glories.

The A3s, though, were overshadowed by their A4 successors, which monopolised all the top jobs. *Flying Scotsman* the engine rarely, if ever, hauled the 'Flying Scotsman' train in BR days.

During the post-war period, *Flying Scotsman* was just another of BR's A3s and did very little of any note. In fact, with better track, better signalling and less traffic, the pre-war racehorses could probably have improved on their speed exploits but to BR, economics and efficiency were more important. The element of competition had gone and BR had no interest in proving that its older engines were faster than its own new designs. Before long the future was going to be diesel anyway.

Perhaps the most positive move, though, was the fitting of a double chimney in 1958 which transformed its performance at the ripe old age of almost 40.

In LNER days, Gresley carried out numerous experiments with his A1 and A3 class, one of which was the fitting of a double chimney and Kylchap double blastpipe to No 2751 *Humorist* in 1937. These had first been tried on the later A4s, *Mallard* having been built with a double chimney, and the earlier engines eventually converted.

The

KYLCHAP

The 'Kylchap' exhaust system originated with the Finnish engineer Kylala, and was perfected by Andre Chapelon, the premier French locomotive designer.

Gresley consulted Chapelon regarding the fitting of the blastpipes to his locomotives and the optimum dimensions. The blastpipe is a hole above the cylinders which allows the steam to escape through the smokebox to the chimney. If the hole is too small, the steam cannot escape quickly enough, so back pressure builds up and slows the engine down. The precise size of the hole is critical to a steam engine's performance, and any double blastpipe design will assist by doubling the speed at which steam can escape.

The Kylchap system is much more complicated, though, with a series of cowls fitted between the blastpipe top and the chimney.

The last four A4 streamliners, including *Mallard*, were built with double chimneys and Kylchap double blastpipes, after experiments on an A3. But, despite the obvious improvements in performance and economy, these were not adopted as standard by the LNER. Appropriately enough, the engine selected for most of the experiments was No 2751 *Humorist*, and some of the smokebox modifications were more comical than effective. These experiments had actually started with the engine still in single-chimney form but, when all the experiments failed, the double chimney and Kylchap were fitted and these were more successful. One drawback was a very soft exhaust, totally different to the loud bark of a single-chimneyed Gresley engine and which could seriously affect the driver's forward visibility.

It was not until the late 1950s, after numerous experiments and negotiations between locomotive depots, particularly King's Cross, and the main works at Doncaster, that a decision was made to convert the rest of the A4s to the double-chimney arrangement. The cost was £200 per engine and, apart from the much more free-running engine, there was a saving in coal of 7lb per mile. Perhaps surprisingly, the rebuilding programme immediately continued with the A3s being treated, at a cost of £153 per engine for a saving of 6lb per mile.

Flying Scotsman received its double chimney in December 1958. Drifting smoke was still a problem but BR was so impressed with the economies obtained that it seems surprising it was so slow in addressing this issue. One, No 98 *Humorist*, the unique double-chimneyed engine for many years, did get smoke deflectors in A1/A2 style in 1947, but little is known of why they were not later adopted widely. The eventual solution is probably one of the most bizarre chapters in the story of British steam traction.

Right: In its final BR condition, with double chimney and smoke deflectors, No 60103 *Flying Scotsman* heads an up express through Hitchin in 1962. COLOUR-RAIL

LNER Pacific tenders

Gresley's A1s had been built with eight-wheel tenders in GNR style with coal rails. In fact these were a little too big at first and turntables had to be extended to accommodate them. *Flying Scotsman* even had to borrow a six-wheel tender for the second Wembley Exhibition in 1925 as it was too long with its normal eight-wheeler.

For the non-stop runs to Newcastle and Edinburgh, new tenders were built with corridors along the side, easily distinguishable as they were much taller, without coal rails. The A1s and A3s with corridor tenders kept them only until new A4s took over all the non-stop runs in 1937. However, new corridor tenders were built for some of the A4s, which were streamlined themselves, and some A4s had new streamlined non-corridor tenders. The A1s and A3s that lost their corridor tenders received new, non-streamlined but high-sided ones, and there was an element of tender-swapping after this, and a small number of A3s could always be seen with high-sided, but non-corridor tenders. *Flying Scotsman* was one of the engines with the high-sided tender throughout from 1927, and the refitting of a corridor tender in 1963 did not, therefore, dramatically alter the engine's appearance.

There had been some further half-hearted experiments with tiny deflectors alongside the chimneys but with little success, but it was Peter Townend, shedmaster at King's Cross, who suggested the fitting of smoke deflectors in the style adopted widely by the Deutsches Bundesbahn. A photograph of a German Pacific was sent to Doncaster Works, some deflectors were designed and manufactured and tried out on an A3, and they worked. Not only did Doncaster start fitting them as A3s passed through works, but a further batch was manufactured and sent to King's Cross to be fitted at the depot.

It was late in the day, though, and not all A3s even received double chimneys. Of those that did, several never actually acquired the smoke deflectors. *Flying Scotsman* was fitted with its smoke deflectors in December 1961, and carried them for just over 12 months.

There is no doubt though, that the double chimney and Kylchap exhaust system, transformed the performance and economy of both the A4s and A3s and although the streamlined Pacifics simply continued much as before, the A3s, *Flying Scotsman* included, which had been relegated to the slightly less arduous main line jobs for many years, found themselves back on 'top-link' duties again, for the last year or two of their 40-year careers. In fact, operations changed quite drastically towards the end of steam, and the traditional engine-changes were largely abolished. A3s and A4s started to work throughout between King's Cross and Newcastle on a far-more-regular basis, something which the A3s had not done since the A4s took their top jobs in 1935.

End of the
A3s

In 1955, BR announced its modernisation plan, a major part of which was the elimination of steam traction. In the post-war era, trains on Britain's fastest main line were still being hauled by steam engines designed more than 30 years earlier, soon after the end of the First World War. *Flying Scotsman* and the A3 class may have been overshadowed by the streamlined A4s on the top duties, but the later Peppercorn Pacifics had merely assisted them, never replaced them, and the even-newer BR Standard designs, such as the Britannia Pacifics, were no competition at all.

Diesels, though, were a threat. Even Gresley had looked into converting to diesel and had visited Germany to travel on the 'Flying Hamburger' diesel express before the war, only to conclude that steam could do anything diesel could do.

Britain was, in fact, rather short-sighted in this respect. The USA was largely dieselised early in the 1950s and most European countries used modern traction quite widely well before Britain. Even after the 1955 announcement, it would be nearly 10 years before steam's supremacy could really be said to have ended in Britain.

In *Flying Scotsman's* case, the first competition came when a few English Electric type 4 1Co-Co1 diesel-electrics were introduced on the East Coast Main Line in 1958, but they were no more powerful, and perhaps rather less reliable. The English-Electric Deltic Type 5 Co-Cos were a more serious matter but only 22 were built as they were phenomenally expensive, but they were able to replace all the A4 streamliners, so it only needed another class of powerful and reliable diesels to arrive in quantity, and that would spell the end for all the LNER Pacifics. That class was the Brush/Sulzer Type 4 Co-Co, the first of which, D1500, started work on the ECML in 1961.

The naming of the King's Cross Deltics after Doncaster winners was a good way of continuing the tradition that was effectively started by *Flying Scotsman*, but *Crepello* and *Ballymoss* would never become household names. The public were far more interested in fast cars and aeroplanes now, not railway engines.

On 7 December 1959, No 60104 *Solario* became the first A3 Pacific to be withdrawn from service to be scrapped, from King's Cross shed, after suffering accident damage, but it was to be another two years before the second one was withdrawn, this time No 60085 *Flamingo*, from Carlisle (Canal) shed. Several A3s were allocated here for working the ex-North British Waverley route to Edinburgh. In later years, A3s even found themselves working over the Settle & Carlisle route between Leeds and the border city, one of the few instances where the class was ever seen away from the traditional LNER routes they were designed for.

From then on, withdrawals accelerated and, on 14 January 1963, No 60103 itself was withdrawn from King's Cross shed after running 2,076,000 miles. *Flying Scotsman's* last run for BR was on the 1.15pm from King's Cross to Leeds as far as Doncaster, attracting considerable media interest. By now, dieselisation was taking effect rapidly and, in May 1963, King's Cross shed closed to steam completely, with a virtual ban on steam being enforced south of Peterborough.

It proved impossible to stop occasional steam workings because of diesel failures, and in 1964, A3 No 60106 *Flying Fox* worked what proved to be the last steam-hauled up 'Flying Scotsman' into King's Cross, after the failure of a Deltic diesel, losing only two minutes on the schedule.

The remaining A3s in England in 1964 were relegated largely to stand-by duties, particularly at Darlington, with a handful at New England shed, Peterborough, that worked occasional parcels, freight and relief passenger trains. On 26 December 1964, the last three English A3s were withdrawn from New England and Nos 60062 *Minoru*, 60106 *Flying Fox* and 60112 *St Simon* went for scrap. They had their final fling on railtour duties, with both No 60106 and 60112 hauling trains from Waterloo, one recording 108mph through Micheldever.

The A3s were still active in Scotland into 1965, though, mainly working from Edinburgh over the Waverley route, usually on goods trains. On 17 January 1966, the last A3 Pacific in BR service was withdrawn – No 60052 *Prince Palatine*, after a farewell railtour from Edinburgh to Carlisle. It was not the last to he scrapped, though, but, when No 60041 *Salmon Trout* was broken up in September 1966, this left just one of the 78 A3s still in existence.

Gresley's A3 Pacifics did not disappear from the East Coast Main Line though. Even by the time the last English A3s were withdrawn from regular service, *Flying Scotsman*, already the most famous of them all, which had been withdrawn nearly two years earlier, could occasionally still be seen, though not at King's Cross, and it presented a rather different appearance than most people were used to by then.

Top: In its final condition and to New England depot's usual standard of cleanliness, one of the last three Gresley A3s to work for BR in England, No 60062 *Minoru*. TERRY ROBINSON

Middle: The last A3 Pacific to be withdrawn from regular service by BR, No 60052 *Prince Palatine*. COLOUR-RAIL

Middle: On its last run for BR, the 1.15pm to Leeds, No 60103 *Flying Scotsman* prepares to depart from King's Cross on 14 January 1963. COLOUR-RAIL

ALAN PEGLER

Scotsman's saviour

There could very easily have been no A3s left at all, if it had not been for Nottinghamshire businessman Alan Pegler, the first of several larger-than-life characters to have become involved with *Flying Scotsman* after its withdrawal from service.

Pegler had seen it at the British Empire Exhibition at Wembley in 1924, and it had left a lasting impression on the young lad such that, 40 years later, when he felt able to save the engine from being scrapped, he went ahead and bought it from British Railways for £3000. He perhaps had a slight advantage, having served as a part-time member of the British Railways Board.

Alan Pegler was not new to steam preservation nor to organising special trains on BR; he had been behind the operation of the two preserved Great Northern Atlantics from York Museum on specials from King's Cross in 1953. He had also been more than just a founder member and prime mover in the campaign to reopen the Ffestiniog narrow gauge railway in North Wales, which from very small beginnings in 1955 had already grown into a major tourist attraction by 1963, and was to progress to even greater heights. Pegler actually bought the railway himself, vested it in a trust to avoid legal complications, and has remained very much involved ever since.

Part of Pegler's deal with BR was that the engine would be overhauled at Doncaster Works, returned to LNER single-chimney form, though still as an A3, and repainted

into LNER apple green livery as No 4472. In fact, at this time it is doubtful if BR would have allowed it to remain in BR livery in private hands. Pegler not only arranged for the engine to be allowed to haul special trains on the national network, which was not an entirely new concept, but he entered into a legally-binding written agreement with BR for a term of three years, later extended to eight years, a unique contract which no other engine owner was ever privileged to obtain. The deal did not quite extend to his driving his own engine on these tours, as the unions felt that this could threaten their members' jobs.

With Doncaster Works still overhauling steam engines on a daily basis, the job did not take long, and a partially-unpainted single-chimney A3 was given a couple of test runs to Peterborough before entering the paint shop for the final touches. The engine was certainly not returned to original condition, but the single chimney enabled the smoke deflectors to be removed and it certainly looked very different to the engine which had hauled the 1.15pm King's Cross-to-Leeds on 14 January. A major alteration that did not radically alter its appearance was the new tender, a corridor-fitted one transferred from the recently withdrawn A4 No 60034 *Lord Faringdon*, which no longer needed it, but which would no doubt be useful in the future.

On 26 March 1963, No 4472 *Flying Scotsman* emerged from the works, looking as good as new, and on 16 April Alan Pegler formally took possession of what was to become his pride and joy.

With steam traction still in everyday use in most parts of the country, *Flying Scotsman* ran more or less like any other steam engine operated by BR, although its runs tended to be longer than most steam duties were by that time. It certainly reached parts of the country it had never seen before but, as steam was rapidly phased out, crucial infrastructure was equally quickly removed, particularly water columns and water troughs. About 80 miles is the normal prudent limit with one tenderful of water, and a quick five-minute top-up from a column is then the normal practice, as messing about with fire hydrants, pumps, road tankers and long lengths of hosepipe is time-consuming and inconvenient.

The first public outing for the preserved No 4472 was from Paddington to Ruabon on a special bound for the Ffestiniog Railway. *Flying Scotsman* was already famous for its exploits 40 years earlier; now it was going to be seen in parts of the country never before visited by a Gresley Pacific. The A3 found its way to Wales, to Scotland, and to the South Coast. One of the Welsh visits was one of the most notable, on 13 November 1965, when No 4472 reached Cardiff from Paddington in 2hr 17min, a record for steam traction.

The eventual solution to the water problem was the acquisition of a second tender, which was actually another corridor one from another newly withdrawn A4, in this case No 60009 *Union of South Africa*, which was also subsequently preserved and acquired a replacement tender.

In September 1966, *Flying Scotsman* emerged from works with two tenders, its first outing in this guise being from Lincoln to Blackpool, a route where the second tender was not really necessary. The second tender carried the number 4472, and the cabsides now carried the LNER coat-of-arms, just as in the Wembley Exhibition of 1924..

A few weeks later, No 4472 was able to return to King's Cross for the first time in two years. Without doubt, the most inconvenient removal of watering facilities was at Peterborough, and without either the platform-end columns or the troughs at Werrington, just to the north,

there was simply no water to be had at just the point it was needed, 76 miles out of the 'Cross'.

Flying Scotsman worked hard for its living, and proved very reliable. June 1967 saw the 40th anniversary of the first King's Cross-to-Newcastle non-stop express, a train that was not, in fact, hauled by *Flying Scotsman*. However, it was an anniversary that ought to be marked by a rerun.

The second tender now gave the engine a range of more than 200 miles without stopping, but nowhere near enough to get to Newcastle. It tends to be forgotten now that, although diesels took over from steam, they still used steam to heat their trains, and diesel classes were actually fitted with water scoops so that they could top up their train heating boiler water tanks from water troughs. A select few troughs had remained in use to avoid diesels having to make unnecessary station stops to take water, and the ones located at Scrooby, Wiske Moor and Lucker remained in use on the ECML.

No 4472 did not make Newcastle non-stop this time but it set the scene for the big one the following year.

Circumstances changed in the meantime. By 1967 *Flying Scotsman* had been joined on the main line by other privately-owned engines and, in the autumn, the East Coast Main Line saw eight weekends of steam, featuring not just No 4472, but its streamlined partner, A4 No 4498 *Sir Nigel Gresley*, and a GWR rival, 4-6-0 No 7029 *Clun Castle*. Tours ran steam-hauled from King's Cross to Newcastle or Carlisle and return, using one of the three locomotives in each direction, but *Flying Scotsman* was the star. With its two tenders, it was the only one able to handle the King's Cross-to-Peterborough leg of the longer tours, and both the other engines were restricted to running north of Peterborough only.

Clun Castle did make it to King's Cross twice, but only on shorter runs to York, and it had to leave its train at

Above: *Flying Scotsman* attracted large crowds wherever it went. During the 1967-1972 BR steam ban, Tyseley in Birmingham was one of the few places where main line steam engines could operate, but only over a few hundred yards of track. Only *Flying Scotsman* was allowed actually to haul trains on the main line, and had arrived at the head of a railtour.
TERRY ROBINSON

Top: Everywhere the engine went, it attracted crowds of onlookers and photographers. The 'North Eastern' railtour passes Steeton & Silsden, near Keighley, on 29 June 1969. JEFF COLLEDGE

Below: *Flying Scotsman* always attracted media attention. A film crew interview the driver as the engine is prepared for a run from King's Cross. TERRY ROBINSON

Peterborough for an hour each time and run two miles to New England for water. Even so, soon after the end of regular steam, there were already areas where the operation of privately preserved steam was proving almost impossible.

It was hardly surprising when, at the end of October 1967, BR issued a statement that it was not prepared to continue to operate privately-owned steam locomotives on any of its routes – *Flying Scotsman* excepted, of course – Pegler's written contract still had four years to run.

But it was not on a totally steamless British Railways that *Flying Scotsman* had what many consider to be its finest hour. BR's last steam engines were still soldiering on in the north-west of England, although their area of operation was contracting and, after 11 August, there would be no more. It was a few months before this that No 4472 attempted the impossible.

On 1 May 1968 it was the 40th anniversary of the first King's Cross-to-Edinburgh non-stop service, a train that *Flying Scotsman* itself had hauled at the tender age of five. Could it be done again? Alan Pegler must have had some very good friends in some very high places to have even dared to suggest it. But, sure enough, at 10am on 1 May 1968, No 4472 set off from King's Cross as it had done countless times before, this time alongside the Deltic-hauled 'Flying Scotsman', and reached Edinburgh 7hr

45min later without having stopped en route. The train had miraculously been allowed to crawl over a broken rail near Doncaster. *Scotsman* had picked up far too little water from water troughs which were only half-full, and the signalman at Berwick-on-Tweed had sent the train into the loop where a road tanker full of cool refreshing water was waiting. The brave decision was made to press on, though; the signalman getting the message and allowing the train through the loop and back on the main line without the wheels having stopped turning – just. Expert driving saw the train coast the last few miles into Edinburgh Waverley and a hero's welcome, with barely a drop of water left in either tender. And, if that was not enough, the exercise was repeated southbound three days later.

It could be said that any engine with two tenders could have achieved this, and the real achievement was that of the many people involved who made it possible. But it was the fact that *Flying Scotsman* became famous for the achievement in 1928, which was a huge media event itself, an event in which the engine's instantly-recognisable name played such a major part, that made the 1968 attempt an even bigger media show.

The BBC were on board and the 60-minute programme that resulted was shown on TV every Christmas for years afterwards.

Little could follow the Edinburgh non-stop, of course. *Flying Scotsman* visited the north-west to play a small part in the run-up to steam's final curtain in the summer of 1968, although it perhaps wisely stayed away for the very end in August.

It did, though, achieve one last honour, being the last steam engine to run over the rival West Coast Main Line route over Shap summit in June 1969.

The years from 1963 to 1969 should probably be regarded as *Flying Scotsman*'s golden years as a preserved locomotive, as Alan Pegler continued to run packed trains over all parts of the British Railways system.

But, as much of this period was a time when BR themselves were still operating steam, albeit in ever-decreasing numbers, even No 4472 is now widely remembered as having been just a privately-owned steam engine hauling railtours back in steam days.

In reality, though, it was much more than this. It had been a legend for 40 years while in everyday service; now it was just starting to do it all over again – and more!

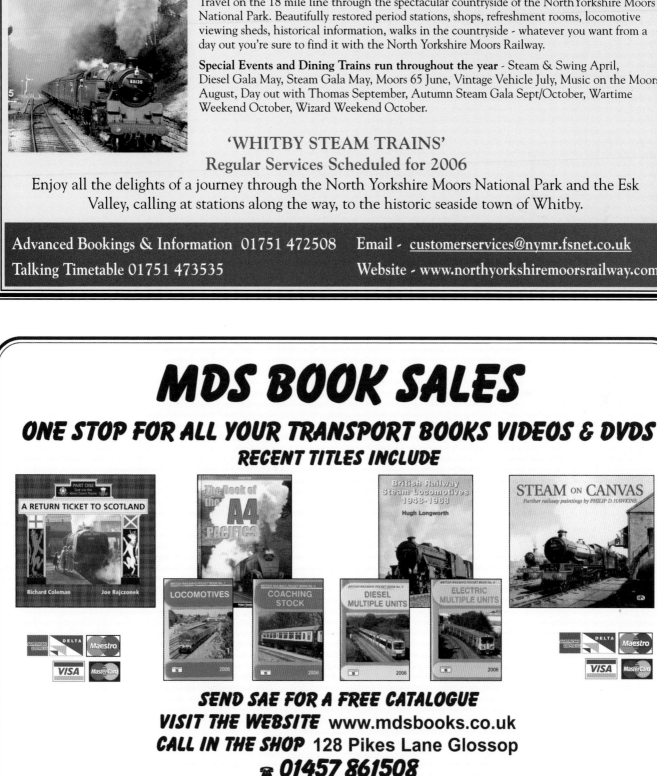

THE NATIONAL
COLLECTION

It is often argued that *Flying Scotsman* should have been officially preserved by British Railways when it was withdrawn from service, and that its acquisition by the National Railway Museum in 2004 was 41 years too late.

Locomotives have been preserved both officially and by private individuals or societies since some of the early locomotives, such as *Locomotion* and *Rocket*, were presented by their owners to local museums in the 19th century.

Preservation remained largely official, ie by the railway companies themselves, with particularly historic engines simply put to one side at Doncaster or Crewe Works, for example, rather then being scrapped, although unfortunately several were later scrapped, particularly during wartime. Although a small number of engines was put on display, such as the Furness Railway 0-4-0 *Coppernob* at Barrow-in-Furness, the first railway museum to be opened was that at York, by the LNER, following the Stockton & Darlington centenary parade in 1925.

Flying Scotsman missed that event and another A1, No 2555, attended, being named *Centenary* in commemoration, a rare exception to the racehorse theme. Private preservation really started when the Stephenson Locomotive Society bought ex-London Brighton & South Coast Railway 0-4-2 No 214 *Gladstone* in 1927, but there was no intention of running it, and the old engine went into the museum at York.

It was not until early BR days that another railway museum opened, at Swindon, and preservation of locomotives began to gather pace after nationalisation. Private preservation also took off after the Second World War, with first the Talyllyn, then the Ffestiniog Railway being reopened in Wales.

The first standard gauge steam railways to reopen were the Bluebell and the Middleton Railway in Leeds, both in 1960, but a year earlier, private preservation had already made a major leap forward. Two standard gauge tank engines were purchased privately from BR and one of them, a Great Northern Railway J52 0-6-0ST, was set to work hauling occasional main line railtours, setting a precedent that larger engines might follow.

BR had found itself with quite a large collection of preserved steam engines, some restored and some not, and some on display and some not. As a result of BR's modernisation plan, and the imminent end of steam, a list was published by the British Transport Commission in 1961 of existing preserved engines, and ones which were to be preserved, to ensure that the widest possible cross-section of British steam locomotive designs could be seen by future generations.

The list was compiled quite scientifically so that, as far as possible, there would be an example of each pre-Grouping and pre-nationalisation railway, at least one from each of the major Chief Mechanical Engineers, and one of each different wheel arrangement. In fact, it was too late in some cases as, for example, no Cambrian Railways engine remained in existence, nor any 4-4-4 tanks. Nevertheless, there were avoidable omissions, although relatively minor ones.

If there is any criticism with the benefit of hindsight, it is the fact that it was too scientific, and little regard was paid to fame and fortune, or public appeal. For example, a Gresley streamlined A4 Pacific was quite rightly included on the list, but *Flying Scotsman* was not; it was considered to be just another Gresley 4-6-2 and there was no justification in preserving two of them, however famous it might be.

There was also a policy decision taken not to preserve engines that were no longer in substantially original condition. In fact, the choice of *Mallard*, the fastest A4, as opposed to *Silver Link*, the first, once the fastest, and arguably the best-known class member, was one of the few exceptions to the scientific rule.

Sure enough, though, something larger was soon purchased privately, and it was a Gresley engine, but it was not *Flying Scotsman*.

K4 2-6-0 No 3442 *The Great Marquess* became the first privately preserved tender engine in 1962 but it never had quite the appeal of *Flying Scotsman*, and was not really suited to running long-distance express trains anyway.

The Great Marquess, purchased by Lord Garnock, did run on main line tours in the mid-1960s, and again many years later, when based on the Severn Valley Railway, including a return to its home territory, the West Highland line in Scotland.

The National Collection could never preserve every type of steam engine, but they have been supplemented by a remarkable variety of privately-preserved engines.

What if?

If *Flying Scotsman*'s fame and popularity had earned it a place in the National Collection, would the story have been the same? The answer is undoubtedly no. The National Collection expanded rapidly towards the end of steam, but there was no money to restore all the engines, certainly not to steam. Some officially preserved engines did steam in the late 1950s and early 1960s but, by 1963, there was no interest in restoring any more, and BR wanted to get rid of all steam as quickly as possible.

The museum at Clapham had been opened in 1960, and space was left for *Mallard*, but this was one of very few engines cosmetically restored in the first part of the 1960s. Only when a regional museum expressed an interest was an engine restored, as happened with LNER V2 2-6-2 No 4771 *Green Arrow* in 1962, when there was a real prospect of a museum being opened at Doncaster. Had *Flying Scotsman* been available, it would very probably have been chosen instead, and could even have been a static exhibit at Doncaster for the past 40 years.

The Doncaster museum, like most others, never materialised, so *Flying Scotsman*, even if it had been externally restored like *Green Arrow*, might have gone into storage, or possibly would have been selected for another museum that failed to materialise, at Leicester, and perhaps it might have been lent eventually to a railway or steam centre to be returned to steam, although it might not initially have returned to single-chimney form.

Like *Green Arrow*, it may well have appeared in steam at the Shildon cavalcade in 1975, and would no doubt have become a permanent exhibit in the new National Railway Museum at York, from where it might have made railtour appearances. None of this would have added as much to its fame or popularity with the public, though; its status would be similar to *Green Arrow* or *Duchess of Hamilton*; still a great and popular engine, but not the most famous locomotive in the world.

Above: At Steam town, Carnforth in September 1974, *Flying Scotsman* stands alongside the Gresley engine that the British Transport Commission chose for preservation in preference – V2 2-6-2 No 4771 *Green Arrow*. BRIAN SHARPE

The Buyer's
TALE

Above : In the early days of Pegler's ownership, with one tender and red-backed nameplates, *Flying Scotsman* is seen at Cambridge.
ERIC SAWFORD

Alan Pegler's ownership of *Flying Scotsman* may have ended with his bankruptcy in 1972 but he has taken a close interest in 'the old girl', as he calls it, ever since.

Alan's involvement in railway preservation did not start with *Flying Scotsman*, of course, as he had already saved the Ffestiniog Railway back in 1955. Even now, he is still the railway's president and he took a short break from working on Ffestiniog business when Brian Sharpe called to see him.

The question that had to be asked was why did he buy *Flying Scotsman*?

"It was the colour really."

As a very young lad, Alan had been taken to the British Empire Exhibition at Wembley, where he had seen *Flying Scotsman*. What had left an impression on him was the big, highly polished, bright green engine, compared with the relatively drab, dark Brunswick green Great Western Castle that stood next to it.

Many years later Alan became involved in the family business, the Northern Rubber Company, at Retford and, as a result, had became a part-time member of the Eastern Area of the British Transport Commission, as it was the practice for a couple of local industrialists to be included on the board.

In 1963 when *Flying Scotsman* was withdrawn from

'If I had retained ownership of the engine, I would have donated it to the National Railway Museum by now' – Alan Pegler

service by BR, Alan felt strongly that a non-streamlined Gresley Pacific ought to be preserved. The BTC would not be swayed, though; a streamlined Pacific and a V2 2-6-2 were to be preserved and the BTC felt that was enough to represent Gresley's work in the National Collection. Alan was certainly not alone in feeling that an A3 ought to be saved, but he was the only person who could go to his bank and get the cash to pay for it.

"There was never any question of buying any other engine." Alan bought *Flying Scotsman* to save it from being scrapped, not because he had a desire to own a main line steam engine. But he had not bought it just to save it; he had bought it to keep it running. Did he expect to make money out of it? "My goodness, no!"

Alan not only paid £3000 to buy *Flying Scotsman*, there were then ongoing payments to BR to maintain and operate it, although income from railtours was obviously set against this.

Alan is quite unequivocal. *Flying Scotsman* did not make money, "and anyone who thinks they can make money out of owning a main line steam engine is living in cloud-cuckoo land".

Having become the proud owner of a Gresley Pacific, Alan needed to keep it somewhere, and he used his contacts within BR management to advantage. At the time, Dr Beeching was the BR chairman, and his reorganisation of the railways went beyond pruning the system. BR workshops were being hived off to separate companies. On Alan Pegler's behalf, Beeching's number two, Sir Stuart Mitchell, asked the new works manager at Doncaster if he could accommodate a privately owned steam engine. "The poor chap was just started in a new job, and the BR vice-chairman came on the phone. I don't suppose he could really have said no."

So Alan got a small shed in the corner of Doncaster Works where he could keep his engine.

Clearly the high point of *Scotsman's* first period of main line running in preservation was the King's Cross-to-Edinburgh non-stop anniversary run in 1968. By then, No 4472 had been running with a second tender for a couple of years, but the extra tender had not been purchased with this run in mind. The thinking was that it would make such runs as Leeds-to-Carlisle over the Settle & Carlisle route possible without a water stop.

Even with the two tenders, the Edinburgh non-stop was a close-run thing. Was there any opposition within BR management to such an ambitious undertaking? "No, I simply paid BR up front and, if anyone tried to stop it happening, I never heard of it," said Alan. "In fact, bets were being placed within BR management as to whether we would reach Edinburgh non-stop or not – but I don't think any of them would have nobbled the water troughs.

"If we thought we could not make Edinburgh, we were to whistle as we approached Berwick. Unfortunately, a chap was lying on the platform trying to photograph the train, and the driver whistled at him. This whistle was misinterpreted as meaning we wanted to stop for the emergency water at Berwick, so we were

signalled into the loop. Fortunately we were able to keep going."

The return was much easier: "We found a chap with a key to the water supply at Scrooby, and got him to hold up the ball-cock so the troughs were filled to overflowing. After a good water pick-up, we ran 140 miles to King's Cross and arrived, non-stop from Edinburgh, with 2000 gallons to spare."

It was the publicity surrounding the non-stop run that led to the American trip. It was an old family solicitor who actually suggested it. Alan had contacts in America, though, including Graham Claytor, president of the Southern Railway, but formerly vice-president (law). The law was to be very influential on this trip

Nelson Blount, a disciple of Billy Graham, agreed to sponsor it, but died in a flying accident immediately prior to *Scotsman's* departure from the UK. With hindsight, Alan admits he probably should have cancelled the trip as a result but so many arrangements had been made, everything was in place and everybody was looking forward to it. Being vacuum-braked, the engine had to take its own train. There was a law that restricted 'foreign' locomotives and trains to circus or exhibition trains only on US railroads, so passenger-carrying was out of the question. Alan also took a couple of Pullman cars, which were never part of his train, but he had agreed to deliver them to a museum in Wisconsin, and what better way could there have been?

Soon, the US authorities were saying to Alan: "It's your engine; why don't you drive the goddam thing?"

So, while in Texas, he took a test for the benefit of the appropriate departments of New York State and Ottawa and, subject to supervision by a qualified traction inspector, Alan could finally drive his own engine.

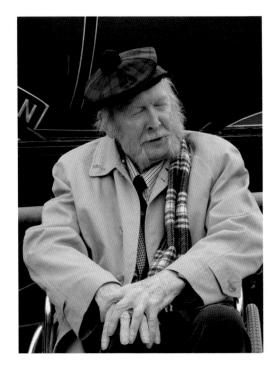

Left: The unmistakable figure of Alan Pegler at the Railfest celebrations at York in 2004.
ROBIN JONES

Right: The crew of *Flying Scotsman* at Boston, about to steam across America.
TERRY ROBINSON

Les Richards, formerly BR North Eastern Region traction inspector, was part of the crew accompanying the train and, under his supervision, Alan reckons he drove No 4472 over approximately 17,000 miles of US and Canadian railroads.

It was the law that finally put a stop to the adventure. "I knew I was going to go bankrupt, but I was enjoying myself," said Alan, but when it was pointed out that he was actually risking arrest, he took the threat very seriously. He was effectively trading while knowingly insolvent and aware that he was running up considerable bills that might never be paid – this is illegal both in the USA and in Britain. Alan knew it had to stop. He returned to Britain and filed for his own bankruptcy while George Hinchcliffe did what he could to secure the engine's future.

William McAlpine had always been a keen supporter of the engine, and acted so quickly that No 4472 was on a boat heading for the Panama Canal before any of the US creditors knew what was happening.

Alan lost everything, but he worked his passage across the Atlantic as a ship's entertainer, a career he took to very quickly, as P&O even asked him to do it again. He is proud he was able to discharge himself from bankruptcy relatively quickly and "with creditors receiving a reasonable proportion of their money". He is also proud to have obtained his Equity card at the age of 60.

Is he pleased that *Flying Scotsman* is now at the National Railway Museum at York, preserved as part of the National Collection? "Yes, undoubtedly. It is where it always should have been."

In fact, he is happy to be quoted as saying that, if he had cancelled the American tour and retained ownership of the engine, he would have donated it to the museum by now. He feels the engine's future as a working engine is much more secure in the museum's hands.

GREAT RAILWAY ADVENTURES 2006
SUPERB ESCORTED TOURS THROUGHOUT THE WORLD
New Brochure now available including a selection of our early 2006 tours.

Contact us for railway touring holidays with chartered steam locomotives hauling our own charter trains plus service trains. You too could see the remaining steam locomotives in action worldwide. (Visit China and Cuba, the last strongholds of steam, before it's too late!). Join famous charter trains in Europe, South America and Asia. There are train journeys in the UK too with vintage steam and diesel haulage.Our train holidays offer railway enthusiasts all the nostalgia of steam, whilst partners enjoy 4 star hotels and the cultural visits en route.For information on programme lists, all future tours - including tours added since the brochure was printed - call or visit our site.Why not visit our site for past tour reports which are first hand accounts.

STEAM TO MANDALAY
14-29th January 2006

This will be our fourth tour to Myanmar (Burma) a remote and fascinating land, where some steam is still used for freight and occasional passenger workings. Extensive cultural programme included. Special steam hauled train from Yangon to Bago - Mottana - Mandalay - Bagan; Mandalay to Madaya; Mandalay to Maymo; and Bagan to Kaukpadeung; featuring ST tank, YD Mikado, YB and YC class Pacifics; all former Indian Railway designs. Plenty of Temples. Irrawaddy River cruise. We have also arranged for those interested an extension to the Burma Mines, an adventure into the northern part of Burma, a trip not for the faint hearted!

HILL STATIONS OF INDIA
11th February - 1st March 2006

This is the perfect way to see India - a mystical place with many contrasts and cultural differences. We travel on some of the most famous steam railways including the Darjeeling Himalayan Railway and the Nilgiri Rack Railway. Travel onboard the 'Fairy Queen' - oldest running steam locomotive from Delhi to Alwar. Steam train to Shimla. Visit the National Railway Museum and the Taj Mahal - a world famous sight. We have a planned main line run with a WP class steam locomotive to Rawari Museum. Visit to a tiger reserve including a jeep safari. Direct British Airways flights from London Heathrow.

VICEROY SPECIAL
4th-16th March 2006

After six hugely successful years, this tour is still as popular as ever, we travel to Kandy to visit the famous Temple of the Tooth, have a tour of Anduraolhapura and travel from Kandy to Nanu Oya - one of the great railway journeys of the world. We again try to recreate some of the atmosphere of the British Raj, with our special charter of the Viceroy Special train steam hauled throughout our journeys with four British built Edwardian steam locomotives of the classic 4-6-0 type. The train itself will consist of two very comfortable lounge cars, a restaurant and bar coach. Sri Lanka (formerly Ceylon) has some very beautiful scenery with rain forests and cascading waterfalls, leafy tea plantations and herds of Indian elephants to be seen in their natural habitat, we visit the Elephant Orphanage at Pinnawela. For those wishing to unwind and relax at the end of the tour we offer a beach extension at the Blue Oceanic Hotel until the 18th March.

CUBA STEAM SAFARI
9th-24th March 2006

On this tour we offer real steam on a Paradise Island; fantastic white sandy beaches, a rich colourful culture, impressive colonial architecture and also many steam locomotives over eighty years old (20 of which are in daily use during the sugar cane harvest 'Zafra').

We will have a main line steam charter from Moron - Ciego-de-Avilla - Jucaro - Manzanilo - Bayamo - Santiago - Guantanamo.

Wonderful Rafael Freyre narrow gauge system, charter railcar from Havana to Holguin and from Santiago to Moron. We will be recreating the experience of loaded sugar cane trains steam hauled from the fields to the mills.

Cuba has been in a time warp since the 1950's so you can expect to see plenty of old American automobiles Pontiacs, Studebakers, Buicks and Chevy's.

This could possibly be the last chance to see working steam in Cuba as progress is now rapid and with progress comes change!

Direct Virgin Atlantic flights from London Gatwick to Havana and return.

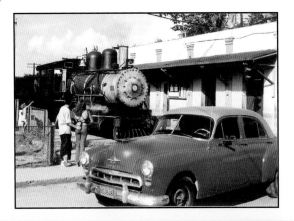

Our brochure is published annually and we would be pleased to send you a copy

The Railway Touring Company
14A Tuesday Market Place, Kings Lynn, Norfolk PE30 1JN
Tel: 01553 661500 Fax:01553 661800
Email: enquiries@railwaytouring.co.uk • Website: www.railwaytouring.co.uk

OVER THE POND

What could follow a London-to-Edinburgh non-stop run, 40 years on from the first, but now on an all-diesel route? There was one more challenge, though: just as other celebrities, such as The Beatles and Oasis, once they become stars at home, then feel obliged to conquer America, Gresley's A3 Pacific No 4472 set out to do just that.

Flying Scotsman emerged from an overhaul at the Hunslet Engine Company in Leeds but, after a few more runs, went into Doncaster Works to be fitted with a bell, a large chime whistle and a cowcatcher. The cowcatcher was out-of-gauge for BR, so it was temporarily removed and, on 31 August 1969, No 4472 had one last run from King's Cross to Newcastle before setting off on its biggest adventure yet.

The plan was for the locomotive to tour the United States and Canada, hauling a nine-coach exhibition train promoting British industry. To say that this plan was ambitious is something of an understatement. American railroads were never nationalised, so No 4472 would have to run on several companies' tracks. Steam was eliminated much earlier than in Britain, and main line steam preservation was virtually non-existent in

the 1960s. There were few qualified steam crews and no steam infrastructure. Steam firemen with any knowledge of coal-fired engines would be even more thin on the ground. Even passenger trains were few and far between, and the engine would have to run colossal mileages on lines that only ever witnessed the passage of multi-engined container trains.

Flying Scotsman left Liverpool Docks on 19 September aboard the MV *Saxonia* for the 10-day journey to Boston, Massachusetts.

Diesel and electric piloting was necessary some of the time but nevertheless *Flying Scotsman* immediately started to hit the headlines. The crew who accompanied the engine had to do everything, and that included driving it, something even Alan Pegler had not achieved (officially) on BR.

The initial tour, starting in Boston on 8 October 1969 and heading south down the eastern seaboard via New York and Washington to Atlanta proved a great success, and No 4472 travelled on to Slaton, Texas for the winter. The Southern Railroad was particularly pro-steam and co-ordinated the tour programme with the assistance of four other railroads. The engine proved reliable, and there were no reports of it delaying freight

Below: *Flying Scotsman* **at Doncaster Works carrying the chime whistle, bell and cowcatcher needed for operation in North America.**
TERRY ROBINSON

trains on long, single-track lines.

A similar tour was then planned for 1970, covering middle America and crossing the border into Canada on 20 August 1970. This was less successful as the British Government was now actively discouraging companies from supporting the train, considering that the steam engine was giving a bad impression of British industry. The BR anti-steam attitude of the time had clearly spread even higher.

But *Flying Scotsman* pressed on and completed the second stage of the tour, its owner thoroughly enjoying himself, even though he knew it could only end in bankruptcy. After almost a year out of action, this time spent in the roundhouse at Spadina shed, Toronto, there was a glimmer of hope that the financial position could be salvaged by a period on show in San Francisco, starting with a trade fair known as 'British Week'.

It was a 4500-mile journey from Toronto to San Francisco, on routes that had not seen a steam engine since the early 1950s. In more recent years, main line steam has made a spectacular comeback on some very long-distance excursions in North America, and effectively it was *Flying Scotsman* that paved the way for these, by proving that it was still possible. If only the train could have carried passengers, there might have been no financial problems, but it was found to be illegal to do so.

In September 1971, No 4472 set off from Toronto for San Francisco. Crossing the Rockies in Canada, it ran short of coal and was assisted by five diesels at one point. It crossed the Columbia River at Wishram, spending some time on tracks once owned by the Great Northern Railroad. On through the Deschutes Canyon and Bend, Oregon, *Scotsman* then steamed down the spectacular Feather River Canyon route of the Western Pacific Railroad, once used by the 'California Zephyr'. On March 18, No 4472 started a season of weekend passenger trips on the San Francisco Belt Railroad, the first steam and the first passengers the line had seen since the Second World War.

After a promising start, standing in a prime position at Fisherman's Wharf, the train was forced to move to a much less satisfactory site and income dried up. Bankruptcy was now inevitable, and Alan Pegler even had to borrow the money for the air fare back to London to file the petition himself. Perhaps his greatest achievement under the circumstances was that he managed to return to San Francisco and arrange for the safe keeping of *Flying Scotsman*, at a US Army base at Stockton, near Sacramento.

Alan's only chance of returning to Britain then was to work his passage on a ship, and he started a new career as an entertainer on board a P&O cruise ship, a career that lasted seven years and enabled him to discharge himself from bankruptcy.

Top: *Flying Scotsman* **in the USA at night.**
TERRY ROBINSON

Top: No 4472 is piloted by a Penn Central Railroad GG1 Class electric at New Rocelle in the New York area.
TERRY ROBINSON

Middle: *Flying Scotsman* at New York alongside a Budd electric railcar.
TERRY ROBINSON

Bottom: Almost a British scene at Boston at the start of the tour as No 4472 comes face-to-face with a London bus.
TERRY ROBINSON

What if?

Flying Scotsman's rise to fame first time round was virtually assured once it acquired its name, as was its further fame once Alan Pegler had reincarnated it 40 years later, but the engine's story is littered with 'might-have-beens' ever since, and it is interesting to consider what might have happened if... Pegler had not negotiated an agreement to run his engine on BR, taking the form of a legally binding written contract. Pegler's close contact with senior BR management put him in a unique position to achieve this, but BR was careful not to enter into any such agreement with anyone else. Without the agreement, *Flying Scotsman* would have become subject to the October 1967 steam ban and, after a couple of years' enforced idleness, would probably have gone to America anyway, as it had been under consideration for several years.

More interestingly, though, what might have happened if, having the benefit of his unique running agreement on BR, Pegler had not been given the opportunity for the American tour, or if he had turned it down?

No 4472 would no doubt have continued running on BR right up to the end of the contract in 1971.

Coincidentally, it was in that year that GWR 4-6-0 No 6000 *King George V* made its ground-breaking tour of the Western Region which led to the lifting of BR's steam ban. Completely new rules were enforced for steam running from 1972, rules which *Flying Scotsman* was subject to on its return from overseas.

The major difference was that *Flying Scotsman* had simply continued running in much the same way after purchase in 1963 as it had previously, with BR taking full responsibility for its operation on what was still, at least partially, a steam-worked railway system. As steam was phased out in different parts of the country, and steam infrastructure was removed, BR found the operation of *Flying Scotsman*, and the other privately-owned steam engines that briefly saw main line use in the 1960s, progressively more difficult.

In reality, by 1969, even No 4472 was quite restricted as to where it could actually run, only its second tender making it a viable proposition at all. Had *Flying Scotsman* still been operating in Britain in 1971, *King George V*'s experimental runs would have been unnecessary, and the engine might not even have been returned to steam by Bulmers. In fact *Flying Scotsman* might have been adopted by Bulmers instead.

With hindsight, BR's main line steam ban was sensible, and *Flying Scotsman*'s temporary emigration was timely. No one really knows whether BR intended the ban to be permanent; no doubt some board members did and some did not. One thing is certain, *Flying Scotsman* would never have become the icon it is now if the ban had remained in force, and we must all be grateful to the many people who worked so hard to get the ban lifted as soon as it was practicable.

Above left: The bell donated by the Southern Railroad to *Flying Scotsman* for the American tour.
JEFF COLLEDGE

Above right: Alan Pegler, in front of the engine's chimney, at Liverpool Docks, just prior to *Flying Scotsman*'s journey to America.
TERRY ROBINSON

'SIR BILL'
McAlpine

William McAlpine, a director of the well-known civil engineering firm Sir Robert McAlpine Ltd, with many railway connections, came to the rescue. The situation called for a man with enthusiasm, money and the right contacts, and Mr McAlpine was just the man for the job.

It was not a case of buying the engine from Pegler; he was bankrupt, so the engine belonged to his creditors. McAlpine had to pay off these creditors quickly and discreetly and get the engine moved out of the USA before either a known creditor took it upon himself to sell No 4472 for scrap, or another creditor surfaced and demanded even more money. McAlpine achieved the seemingly impossible remarkably quickly and, on 19 January 1973, *Flying Scotsman* was his, and was on the MV *California Star* bound for Liverpool via the Panama Canal.

McAlpine was an enthusiast and an owner not only of steam locomotives but of an entire railway, in his garden. Garden railways are not particularly unusual, and some are even full-size narrow gauge systems, but McAlpine's, the Fawley Hill Light Railway, is standard gauge!

Mr McAlpine became Sir William in 1980.

As from 1972, locomotive owners took responsibility for the operation of their engines on main lines. It was their duty to provide BR with an engine in full working order, coaled and watered ready to run, and to ensure that it was coaled, watered and serviced as necessary during the day. All BR did was provide the crew, the train and the track to run on. Pegler had not had to do this initially; he had simply paid BR to run the engine, although a team of volunteers led by George Hinchcliffe had become increasingly involved in its operation. Now, in effect, BR paid the engine owners to hire their engines (only a nominal sum of course).

This was a radically different approach for the post-steam era. Under McAlpine's ownership, *Scotsman* needed a team of willing volunteers to accompany the engine and attend to its every need during the day.

'Sir Bill' McAlpine was one of four millionaire private owners, or part-owners, of *Flying Scotsman*. But his was the most enduring, but at the same time most low-key of them all. Sir Bill never featured on the six o'clock news, posing on the footplate of 'his' engine. He simply owned it, and it continued to do its job, but at times spectacularly. In fact Sir Bill contributed far more to railway preservation than is generally realised, and continues to do so. He gave up ownership of *Flying Scotsman* only because he felt he was getting old, and that its future would be more secure with a younger part-owner at least.

Alan Pegler was 43 when he bought the engine, and he owned it for nearly 10 years; William McAlpine was 36, and he kept it for 20 years. Pete Waterman became involved at 46, for just three years. Dr Marchington, its last private owner, was 40, and his involvement lasted for seven years.

Although McAlpine's ownership was quiet and low-key, it was eventful, and his 20-year involvement saw the engine's fame increase enormously.

Above right: Bill McAlpine did not just buy *Flying Scotsman*. He also collected and restored a number of historic coaches at Carnforth. This train was often used for entertaining corporate clients, sometimes with *Flying Scotsman* at the head. No 4472 passes Bolton, then little changed since steam days, on 28 September 1979, with a McAlpine private charter from Carnforth to Dinting, near Glossop.
BRIAN SHARPE

What if?

If Bill McAlpine had not secured *Flying Scotsman*'s release from the USA by paying off the engine's creditors, those creditors would have sold it eventually, to recover part of their debt. It is perhaps surprising that they did not do so immediately; although possibly this was because the engine was considered to be of little value in the US at the time. Scrap value in Britain might have been £10,000 and in the States probably a similar figure. Although there was a market in railway memorabilia in America, it was nothing compared to the UK today, where a nameplate alone can fetch £60,000. The debts incurred were no doubt way in excess of £10,000, so it would never have been worthwhile for any of the creditors to seize the asset and sell it, as they would have been forced to share the proceeds with everyone else; and, as is the case in most bankruptcies, they might have received the equivalent of .001p-in-the-£1 each. The danger is that it only needs one creditor to threaten to take action and demand a separate deal to undo all that has been achieved.

The engine might have been sold for scrap, or to a private collector, or museum, or to an American preserved railroad. However, the attraction of a British steam engine in America is not all it might be

expected to be. There are two LNER A4 Pacifics preserved the other side of the Atlantic, and neither museum has ever tried to steam its engine in the expectation of picking up rich profits from American tourists.

It was perhaps the tour promoters' over-estimation of the fame of the engine and its money-making potential that caused the venture to fail spectacularly, but it was also the reason why it was possible to save the engine relatively painlessly.

If it had passed into American ownership, like the SS *Queen Mary*, it would have returned to the UK by now. Any private collector would have died eventually, with his collection dispersed. A railroad operating it for profit would have found it uneconomic by comparison with US-built engines and would have offered it for sale. *Pendennis Castle* went to Australia, and SR Schools class 4-4-0 No 30926 *Repton* went to Canada, both as operating engines, but both were sold and repatriated eventually. The same would have been true of *Flying Scotsman*, provided it had not been scrapped. The story may not have been vastly different if Bill McAlpine had not stepped in, but that is not to understate the debt that British steam enthusiasts owe to him.

Scotsman
COMES HOME

Whene *Flying Scotsman* returned to the UK in February 1973, it was to a very different world from the one it had left behind in 1969. The BR ban on main line steam had come into force in October 1967, but No 4472 had been exempt, because of Pegler's binding contract with BR. Now, though, that had expired.

The steam ban had fortunately been short-lived, but *Flying Scotsman* was to be subject to exactly the same rules and regulations that applied to all the other, lesser engines. Just six routes, spring and autumn running only, and no exceptions to the rules.

However, *Flying Scotsman* was still regarded as something of a special case and, if rules could be bent to ensure the engine kept its dignity, they would be. After a year of disuse and weeks standing on the deck of a cargo vessel in Atlantic storms, it was inspected at Liverpool and passed fit to run. *Flying Scotsman* made its way light engine to Derby under its own steam, hardly bothering with technicalities such as 'approved steam routes', and entered the one-time LMS locomotive works for an overhaul. Emerging as good as new in July 1973, it was time for it to start earning its keep as quickly as possible.

Steam remained banned from BR tracks in summer, but again No 4472 at least travelled under its own power, hauling two vintage saloons also acquired by McAlpine, the destination being Paignton, for a busy summer season on the Torbay Steam Railway. It was only when this was successfully completed and main line action could be entertained again in September that the A3 could get back into railtour action, under the new regulations.

Loading gauge

A loading gauge was designed to ensure that people loading open wagons did not stack the goods so high or wide that they would strike overbridges or tunnels. Every goods yard had one, and many can still be seen today. The term is also taken to mean the dimensions of a locomotive or item of rolling-stock. All must be designed to fit comfortably under all bridges and tunnels they are expected to encounter.

The loading gauge on Britain's railway system varies more widely than might be expected, but it is certainly among the smallest in the world. The fact that British steam locomotives hold so many world records is all-the-more surprising, taking into account that they had to be built so much smaller than in every other country.

Broadly speaking, ex-Great Western main lines have the largest loading gauge, especially in terms of width, as they were originally built to 7ft 0¼in gauge. The Great Central London extension also has a generous loading gauge, having been built relatively late and designed to accommodate Continental-sized rolling-stock at a future date. Scottish lines tend to be narrow, and some of the tightest clearances are in Kent.

Flying Scotsman and the other early A1s immediately fell foul of loading gauge problems. They were designed to haul Great Northern Railway expresses between King's Cross and York but, once the GNR was absorbed into the LNER, it would be much more useful if they could run on all LNER main lines. They had to be trimmed slightly to fit under bridges on the North Eastern Railway, and slightly more for the North British routes north of the border.

The LMS main lines have a slightly more generous loading gauge and, once cleared for all LNER main lines, the A1s could run on nearly all main lines in Britain. This has proved particularly useful in more recent years as *Flying Scotsman* has been able to run in most parts of the country. An exception remains Kent, where the only express engines that can be used on most routes are those designed by the Southern Railway.

GWR engines are not generally much taller and wider than their counterparts, although 4-6-0 No 6024 *King Edward I* has been shortened in recent years to give it wider route availability away from GWR main lines. The problem with GWR engines is the wide front buffer beam and the distance between it and the leading driving wheels. The overhang on a sharp curve through a station platform has caused engines to become stuck when away from home territory, even in recent years. Gresley's A1s, although more compact and with much less front-end overhang on curves, still struck platforms on sharply curved Scottish routes. This led to corners being cut out of the buffer beams – just one difference between Gresley's original design and *Flying Scotsman* today.

Loading gauge unfortunately is not constant. Diesels have generally been designed to be 'go anywhere' machines and there have been well-publicised instances where track has been reballasted, reducing clearances to an extent that remains perfectly acceptable for diesels but becomes too tight for many steam engines, and at least three engines have struck bridges in recent years.

In fact BR, Railtrack and Network Rail must be commended for (usually) ensuring that clearances are not reduced, just in case a steam engine ever wants to use the route. There have been occasions when this has not been possible, though, particularly on electrified routes, where there must understandably always be a minimum clearance between the tops of chimneys and wires carrying 25,000 volts.

Axle loading is also a problem, of which the A1s quickly fell foul when built. It is not the total weight of the engine that is the issue, it is the weight carried by each axle, which can vary widely according to where the weight of the engine is concentrated. Gresley was given a maximum figure to work to, but the A1s in practice still exceeded the weight that had been calculated, despite using as many weight-saving ploys as possible. Axle loadings have generally been increased, and *Flying Scotsman* can now run on many routes that would have been unthinkable in days gone by, particularly private heritage lines on quite lightly-engineered branch lines.

For maximum impact, No 4472 teamed up with the engine that had finally managed to break BR's ban, GWR 4-6-0 No 6000 *King George V*, an engine that coincidentally had travelled to America in 1927 and carried a commemorative bell. The train was billed as 'The Atlantic Venturers Express' and ran from Newport to Shrewsbury on 22 September 1973.

No 4472 was then back into promotional duties again. No 6000 was based at Bulmers' cider factory in Hereford, along with an exhibition train formed of Pullman cars. The exhibition train was to tour the country promoting Bulmers' products and, although steam haulage was favoured, *King George V* was 'out of gauge' for the vast majority of the BR system, so *Flying Scotsman* stood in, although still restricted to the 'approved routes', such as York to Scarborough and Newcastle to Carlisle.

Flying Scotsman needed a new home, as Doncaster diesel depot was no longer available. The Hon John Gretton of Stapleford Park, near Melton Mowbray, who had become the owner of *Flying Scotsman*'s one-time arch-rival, GWR 4-6-0 No 4079 *Pendennis Castle*, was setting up a railway centre at Market Overton in Rutland, and this was chosen as *Flying Scotsman*'s home base, at least for the winter months.

Market Overton was at the end of a disused branch line from the East Coast Main Line at Highdyke, north of Stoke Tunnel, which had served ironstone mines. There was a small but fairly modern locomotive shed that had housed the quarry's fleet of industrial diesels. Other engines followed, including the National Railway Museum's ex-Barry scrapyard SR Merchant Navy Pacific No 35029 *Ellerman Lines*, which was to be cosmetically restored but sectioned to show the internal workings of a steam engine, in the new museum to be opened at York. Considerable engineering skills were being established at Market Overton, which would bear fruit in the future.

As a preserved railway, though, the scheme never took off. It was an inconvenient location for main line operations, remote from all the 'approved routes', and would never be suitable in itself as a venue for big engines to stretch their legs. *Flying Scotsman* and *Pendennis Castle* quickly deserted their new home and made for Carnforth in the north-west.

Above: No 4472 *Flying Scotsman* hauls passenger trains again in Britain, for the first time in four years. But it is not on the main line, it is on the privately-owned 25mph-restricted Torbay Steam Railway, a one-time Great Western branch line.
BRIAN SHARPE

'APPROVED'
steam routes

GWR 4-6-0 No 6000 *King George V* toured part of the Western Region in October 1971 with Bulmers' cider train, plus additional coaches, for fare-paying passengers. As a result, BR announced the end of its infamous steam ban, with effect from June 1972.

Operations, though, were to be strictly limited to just six short routes, in spring and autumn only, and for just a few engines based on or near the designated routes.

Gradually, the BR system was opened up to steam, culminating in September 1992 with the whole of the Southern Region, but only at night, but then in daylight from the following year. Busy inter-city routes, especially 25kv overhead electrified territory, remained strictly no-go, and routes were deleted as electrification was extended.

Flying Scotsman joined in from the second half of the 1973 season, and gradually stretched its legs on a fair proportion of the designated routes, often with the first train.

Above right: One of the six original 'approved' routes for steam was the Hope Valley line between Sheffield and Manchester. On a clear autumn afternoon, No 4472 *Flying Scotsman* rounds the curve at Buxworth on 10 November 1984. The train was 'The Fenman', which No 4472 would haul as far as Spalding, the route beyond Sheffield having been given one-off dispensation, as often seemed to happen with this particular engine, which was on its way to the East End for a Royal assignment.
BRIAN SHARPE

In 1972, the original routes were:
Didcot –Tyseley
Newport – Shrewsbury
Carnforth – Barrow-in-Furness
York – Scarborough
Newcastle – Carlisle
Guide Bridge – Sheffield

In 1973, this was expanded to include:
Barrow – Sellafield
Hull – Scarborough
Leeds – Carnforth
Inverkeithing – Dundee

1974 saw the following added:
Basingstoke – Westbury
Edinburgh – Perth – Aberdeen

1975 one-offs for the Rail 150 celebrations at Shildon
Battersby – Whitby
Sheffield – York – Newcastle

In 1976, routes were considerably expanded:
Shrewsbury – Chester
Newcastle – Middlesbrough replaced Newcastle – Carlisle

Leeds – York via Harrogate
Perth – Inverness
Inverness – Kyle of Lochalsh
Sheffield – York
Manningtree – March

1980
Liverpool – Manchester
Manchester – Leeds via Standedge
Manchester – Blackburn – Hellifield

1984
Fort William – Mallaig
Marylebone – Banbury
In 1985, added as one-offs:
Bristol – Plymouth
Gloucester – Swindon
Plymouth – Truro

1986
Salisbury – Yeovil

1987
Glasgow – Fort William
Chinley – Buxton
Machynlleth – Aberystwyth/Pwllheli

Left: *Flying Scotsman* was understandably popular for promotional tours, but even these had to stick to the 'approved' routes. No 4472 passes Kirkstall, running from Leeds to Carnforth on 25 July 1976 with an exhibition train extolling the virtues of Pioneer hi-fi systems.
BRIAN SHARPE

Steamtown,
CARNFORTH

The unremarkable little Lancashire town of Carnforth occupies a unique position in the hearts of British steam enthusiasts, as it was one of the last three BR steam locomotive sheds to operate steam, right up to the last day of scheduled services on 3 August 1968.

By then, a collection of preserved engines was already stored in the yard, with a view to their future use on a steam railway being proposed in the Lake District. The renting of the whole shed and yard after the end of steam was planned to be a temporary arrangement, until the line could be secured and reopened. Further engines arrived, including several LMS 'Black Five' 4-6-0s purchased privately at the end of steam.

The line from Plumpton Junction through Greenodd and Haverthwaite to Windermere Lakeside would have been an excellent proposition for a steam railway, but the revivalists were unable to prevent half the line being swallowed up by the A595 Haverthwaite bypass, severing the remaining section from the BR system. Although many of the Lakeside & Haverthwaite Railway Society members pressed on with the project, and the three-and-a-half-mile Lakeside & Haverthwaite Railway has developed into a very professional and attractive heritage line, Carnforth shed, marketed as Steamtown, also developed into a visitor attraction in its own right, and many of those involved, feeling that the Lakeside branch could never compare with what was originally planned, stayed put, and continued to develop Steamtown.

The lifting of BR's steam ban in 1972, and Carnforth's nomination as a main line steam operating base, sealed the shed's future. It then started to attract more and bigger engines looking for main line action and, as early as 1973, this included *Flying Scotsman*. It was an association that was to last for almost 15 years.

Today, Carnforth shed serves a different, but no less valuable purpose. The railway restoration and engineering side of the business was expanded, and eventually purchased by the West Coast Railway Company, set up by Yorkshire farmer, businessman and steam locomotive owner David Smith.

The engineering business had already dealt with contracts such as the refurbishment of the Pullman coaches for the Venice-Simplon Orient Express. After the privatisation of BR, WCRC became a Train Operating Company in its own right operating, for example, the 'Jacobite' summer steam service between Fort William and Mallaig. The train operating side of the business has also steadily expanded and WCRC now operates the 'Ride the Legend' York-to-Scarborough trains hauled by *Flying Scotsman* during the summer months.

The shed is not now open to the public, though. Its facilities never made it an ideal venue for visitors and its upgrading could never justify the cost. Carnforth, though, still plays a vital part in keeping steam alive on Britain's main lines.

Right: Carnforth shed retained its steam age atmosphere well into the preservation era. On 21 March 1976, *Flying Scotsman* **stands in the yard with Barclay 0-4-0 crane tank** *Glenfield,* **while Dr Peter Beet's German Pacific No 012-104 steams past.** BRIAN SHARPE

Above right: *Flying Scotsman* **stands at Steamtown, Carnforth in April 1992 together with two coaches just outshopped by the Carnforth Railway Restoration Company for the Venice-Simplon Orient Express. It would be almost 20 years before No 4472 could actually haul these coaches on the main line, after it was fitted with air brakes.** BRIAN SHARPE

CUMBRIAN

Coast Express

One of the first routes to be sanctioned by BR for occasional steam operation from 1972 was from Carnforth to Barrow-in-Furness, giving the small fleet of LMS 'Black Five' 4-6-0s preserved there an opportunity to stretch their legs occasionally.

In 1973, the approval was extended farther up the Cumbrian coast to Sellafield and, when *Flying Scotsman* first visited Steamtown at Carnforth in September 1973, it made its first-ever run on this route – the first of what was to be a very large number of runs.

In late 1974, No 4472 returned to Carnforth, this time on a permanent basis, and by now it was permitted to run not only to Sellafield, but south to Leeds. The West Coast Main Line over Shap, and the nearby Settle and Carlisle line remained out-of-bounds, but the Cumbrian Coast line to Sellafield was a very attractive alternative.

The 64-mile route was a reasonable distance and could be covered each way with steam in a day, even with a train originating from Euston, as most railtours did. It is scenic, with the sea on one side and the Cumbrian Fells on the other side all the way. Although it is relatively level, there is a short, sharp climb out of Ulverston one way and Lindal on the return to test the engine.

While Sellafield is not an ideal destination for a day trip, there is also Ravenglass a few miles farther south, where most passengers would alight for a trip on the Ravenglass & Eskdale miniature railway. The engines could be turned at Sellafield on a trangle at the British Nuclear Fuels plant, or alternatively on the Ministry of Defence Vickers gun range system south of Ravenglass. In practice, engines did not take kindly to the curves on either of these triangles and it was usual to use two different engines, with one running light engine tender-first between Carnforth and Sellafield.

Flying Scotsman's appearances on the route grew more frequent and such was its popularity that, on one occasion in May 1976, a railtour comprised no less than 18 coaches. *Flying Scotsman* was honoured with the assistance of LNWR 2-4-0 No 790 *Hardwicke* as far as Ulverston, where more substantial assistance was provided in the shape of LNER B1 4-6-0 No 1306 *Mayflower*.

In July 1978, though, the unthinkable happened and BR itself started to run regular steam trains for the first time in 10 years. It hired *Flying Scotsman*, which had just emerged from an overhaul at Vickers Ltd in Barrow, where it was fitted with its spare boiler, the one Alan Pegler had purchased in 1963. It was, in fact, an A4-type boiler once carried by No 60019 *Bittern*. The train was the 'Cumbrian Coast Express', starting from Blackpool and aimed at holidaymakers. It was steam-hauled from Carnforth to Sellafield and back, using No 4472 one way and LNER A4 Pacific No 4498 *Sir Nigel Gresley* the other. It was to run every Tuesday throughout the summer, but was very quickly expanded to Wednesdays also.

The programme was extended in 1979 and other engines were included, but various circumstances led to what had been a very successful venture being surprisingly short-lived. It did, however, prove that regular timetabled main line steam trains can make money.

Steam operation continued in the form of occasional one-off tours, and was extended again, as far as Maryport, with engines being able to continue light to Carlisle. The trains could go no farther as even BR coaches are out-of-gauge for the Maryport to-Carlisle section.

The regular service was relaunched in a slightly different form in 1987, but this time the train was called the 'Sellafield Sightseer', the destination quite unashamedly being the nuclear power station, which had opened a visitor centre and wanted to improve its public perception.

Again *Flying Scotsman* was part of BNF's marketing 'spin'. The trains were successful, but controversial, attracting not quite the type of media interest that had been envisaged. Unfortunately it virtually spelt the end of steam working on the Cumbrian Coast line, owing to the increased publicity surrounding the perceived health hazards of the area.

Carnforth and the Cumbrian Coast was a long way from Flying Scotsman's normal sphere of operations in its regular service days, but it proved that the engine was nothing if not adaptable, and this proved to be one of the engine's most successful periods in its preservation career.

Top left: *Flying Scotsman* crosses Eskmeals Viaduct, south of Ravenglass, with the 'Cumberland Sausage' railtour on 18 June 1983.
BRIAN SHARPE

Bottom left: No 4472 rounds the curve at Millom with a Carnforth-to-Sellafield train on 7 May 1990.

No 4472 *Flying Scotsman* passes Whitbeck on 30 May 1987 with a 'Sellafield Sightseer' train. The helicopter was being used by a TV company filming the train for a news item on anti-nuclear protests taking place at Sellafield. BRIAN SHARPE

This is
YORK

Flying Scotsman has a long association with the city that is now its permanent home. Gresley designed his A1 Pacifics to run between King's Cross and York and, for all of their working lives, the A1s and later A3s ran mainly on the East Coast Main Line passing through the city.

During its days fitted with a corridor tender, working the Newcastle and Edinburgh non-stops, *Flying Scotsman* would have been an almost daily sight in York but, once the A4s took over the top duties in 1935, No 4472 as a King's Cross engine would rarely have worked north of Grantham.

Only in its very last days, with the benefit of the double chimney and Kylchap, were the Grantham engine changes largely abandoned, and King's Cross A3s used on runs right through to York and Newcastle again.

Once in preservation, up until 1969 the East Coast Main Line remained a favourite route for *Flying Scotsman*, based not far away at Doncaster.

On its return from the USA, though, No 4472 found itself with only a handful of routes to run on and, although York-to-Scarborough was one of them, the engine used the route only once in 1972, hauling the Bulmer's Cider exhibition train. Based at Carnforth from 1974, *Scotsman* was allowed to run to Leeds but no farther. 1975 was a special year, though.

The Stockton & Darlington centenary celebrations took place at Shildon at the end of August, followed by the opening of the new National Railway Museum at York. This led first to a procession of steam engines passing through York en route to and from Shildon but, perhaps better still, a short series of railtours on the East Coast Main Line.

Flying Scotsman made the journey from Carnforth to Shildon on an August Sunday afternoon, hauling just one coach, Bill McAlpine's Caledonian Railway observation car No 41, and piloted by none other than the LNWR's 1892-vintage 2-4-0 No 790 *Hardwicke*. After its appearance at Shildon, when it hauled NER 2-4-0 No 910 in the famous cavalcade, No 4472 returned to Carnforth with a lengthy empty stock train, this time accompanied by GWR 4-6-0 No 6960 *Raveningham Hall*. Two weeks later *Scotsman* returned many of the coaches to York, this time piloted from Carnforth by the National Railway Museum's LNER Gresley V2 2-6-2 No 4771 *Green Arrow*. Nowhere in Britain had seen such a level of steam activity for many years, and it was a strong indication that the new museum at York was about real working steam; it was not going to be just a static collection of inanimate objects.

The four main line railtours in September were planned to feature four different LNER Pacifics, *Flying Scotsman* naturally being one of them. In the event, A4 No 4498 *Sir Nigel Gresley* worked the first one, from

Below: After the Rail 150 cavalcade at Shildon on 31 August 1975, *Flying Scotsman* takes centre stage at Darlington as the engines prepare for the journey home. The supporting cast includes LMS 8F 2-8-0 No 8233 from the Severn Valley Railway, LMS 'Black Five' No 4767 *George Stephenson* from the North Yorkshire Moors Railway, the National Railway Museum's BR 9F 2-10-0 No 92220 *Evening Star* and Carnforth-based LMS Jubilee 4-6-0 No 5690 *Leander*. BRIAN SHARPE

Newcastle to York and back, while the remaining three were shared by the apple green trio of B1 4-6-0 No 1306 *Mayflower*, *Green Arrow* and *Flying Scotsman* in various combinations.

Then, the following year, it was back to normal, although Leeds to York via Harrogate was added to the list of 'approved' routes. *Flying Scotsman* immediately showed that it was still a bit of a special case, by using the main line between Leeds and York instead on 24 April. In fact, running via Harrogate was so inconvenient that the direct route was soon authorised for regular steam, as was the York-to-Sheffield line, giving No 4472 much easier access to York and other

parts of the BR system.

In 1979, after the success of the 'Cumbrian Coast Express' from Carnforth, BR introduced its own 'York Circular' steam service, initially running twice daily between York and Leeds. Steam runs to Scarborough were very occasional, particularly after BR lifted the turning triangle at Filey, but in 1981 the ex-Gateshead shed turntable was installed at Scarborough, paid for by Scarborough Borough Council, and BR itself began running the 'Scarborough Spa Express', a 212-mile York-Harrogate-Leeds-York-Scarborough and return operation, three days a week. Both York and Carnforth-based engines were used, including *Flying Scotsman*.

Above: No 4472 *Flying Scotsman* backs on to the 'Scarborough Spa Express' at York on 29 July 1981. BRIAN SHARPE

Left: *Flying Scotsman* played a starring role in the feature film *Agatha*, filmed at York station in late 1978. Returning to Carnforth on 3 December with an already-heavy train, No 4472 also had to contend with the additional weight of Southern Railway 4-6-0 No 30850 *Lord Nelson*, which was to be restored at Carnforth in time for the 1980 Rainhill cavalcade. Passing Copmanthorpe, *Scotsman* meets a Deltic on a northbound express. BRIAN SHARPE

In 1987, before electrification of the East Coast Main Line, *Flying Scotsman* sets out from York southbound as it had done so many times before. On this occasion though, it was not heading for King's Cross, but Carlisle via Leeds. BRIAN SHARPE

SETTLE & CARLISLE

Below: On 4 July 1987
Flying Scotsman had
one of its longest
runs, a railtour from
Carlisle to York and
back. Late in the
evening, No 4472
climbs what
railwaymen refer to
as the 'Long Drag'
from Settle Junction
to Blea Moor past
Selside. BRIAN SHARPE

On 1 May 1976 LNWR 2-4-0 No 790 *Hardwicke* again teamed up with *Flying Scotsman* for a run with a train of historic coaches to commemorate the centenary of opening of England's most ruggedly spectacular main line and a firm favourite with steam enthusiasts.

It was an absolutely foul day and the train was not allowed actually to run steam-hauled on the S&C itself. It ran steam-hauled from Carnforth to Hellifield, where the engines were removed and were permitted to travel as far as Settle station light engine. This unspectacular event was the first small step towards the return of steam to the route that had been the talk of the enthusiasts' world for years.

The actual problem was that, from the six routes approved for steam in 1972, the list had grown steadily, but inter-city main lines and electrified routes were off-limits. While the West Coast Main Line over Shap would never have been approved anyway, it was electrified in 1974 and this effectively put Carlisle station out of bounds so, although the Settle & Carlisle could well have been given approval in 1974 or 1975, the overhead wires now seemed to preclude it forever.

In every other country in the world, steam has operated on electrified routes without a problem and, as electrification was extended in Britain, there were more and more instances when a steam engine ran into an electrified station. Eventually it was agreed that it was safe to do so, under certain conditions. This was a crucial decision as, without it, steam operation would be extremely limited in Britain today.

At Easter 1978, steam returned to the Settle and Carlisle line, the engine leading the way being *Flying Scotsman*'s smaller sister, V2 2-6-2 No 4771 *Green Arrow*. No 4472 made it up the 1-in-100 southbound to the 1169ft Ais Gill Summit on 16 June that year, with a McAlpine private charter. It was not until September that *Flying Scotsman* hauled a public passenger train on the route. On this occasion two trains ran, using three engines – the A3 together with SR Merchant Navy 4-6-2 No 35028 *Clan Line* and BR 9F 2-10-0 No 92220 *Evening Star*. The trains ran in memory of perhaps Britain's most famous steam photographer, Bishop Eric Treacy, who had collapsed and died at Appleby while photographing *Evening Star* in May.

After a handful of steam trips, the Settle & Carlisle was ruled out for steam traction during 1979 after the collapse of Penmanshiel Tunnel, which resulted in East Coast Main Line expresses using the route.

From 1980, though, steam returned to the Settle & Carlisle on an almost weekly basis with the inauguration of the 'Cumbrian Mountain Express', a train which frequently featured haulage by *Flying Scotsman*. Once the S&C was opened up for steam, it became the favourite route for enthusiasts, engine owners, railtour operators and the public. The threat of closure in the 1980s enhanced its popularity and, since its reprieve, passenger and freight traffic on the line has expanded rapidly, to the extent that it has become quite difficult to fit a relatively slow-moving steam train in between the other traffic.

Above: From 1972 to 1978, steam was not permitted to run in summer, because BR could not spare any coaches at weekends. Steam was not permitted in winter for reasons that are less clear but, from 1979, this restriction was lifted and wintertime steam has been a great success, leading to the return of such spectacular sights as *Flying Scotsman* topping a snowbound Ais Gill Summit on the Settle & Carlisle line on 30 January 1983. BRIAN SHARPE

HAPPY BIRTHDAY!

Scotsman's Diamond Jubilee

Above: Large crowds watch *Flying Scotsman* as it departs from Doncaster on 6 March 1983. These three runs marked the first time in 14 years that the engine had run on part of the route it was built for, at Doncaster 60 years earlier, the Great Northern main line from King's Cross to York. It would be another 16 years, though, before circumstances changed sufficiently for steam to return to the route in its entirety. BRIAN SHARPE

Early 1983 saw the engine's 60th birthday, and considerable rule-bending took place to allow *Flying Scotsman* to celebrate this milestone in an appropriate manner by running on the Great Northern main line. One trip, with the engine hauling the train one way from Grantham to York, was envisaged initially, but demand was such that one run quickly became three and, better still, the engine changing point was altered to Peterborough, allowing the A3 to be reacquainted with Stoke bank for the first time in 14 years.

The actual anniversary of emerging from Doncaster Works was celebrated by a private run from Carnforth to York, but the engine then ran with a couple of coaches to Peterborough late on a Saturday evening, to turn on the loop installed for flyash trains in the 1960s. On three consecutive Sundays from 27 February,

No 4472 took over its well-filled Pullman trains at Peterborough and headed north, the third trip actually running to Carnforth as opposed to York.

The trains were popular with the travelling public but much too popular with lineside observers. While other steam engines attract a good turnout of enthusiasts, not all of whom strictly obey the rules of trespass, but who are generally sensible, *Flying Scotsman* attracts everyone and his dog. Its fame can sometimes be its undoing. Trespass by the public reached almost epidemic proportions and East Coast Main Line expresses had to be stopped while people were cleared from the tracks. All three trains ran without loss of life or limb, on the railway at least, but any thoughts that BR management might have had about permitting steam on inter-city main lines on a regular basis in the future quickly evaporated.

Above: *Flying Scotsman* emerges from Lords Tunnel at South Hampstead, soon after leaving Marylebone. At this point, the engine is crossing over the West Coast Main Line from Euston. BRIAN SHARPE

Below: No 4472 *Flying Scotsman* emerges from White House Farm Tunnel near High Wycombe at sunset on 3 January 1987. BRIAN SHARPE

Steaming back to
'THE SMOKE'

lying Scotsman was built for the King's Cross-to-York main line, and spent most of its main line career based at King's Cross shed. Built at Doncaster and preserved by Alan Pegler at Doncaster, in later years it was regarded as a Yorkshire engine and was regularly seen at York, but it had always been very much a London engine in 'real' steam days.

Visits to London continued up to its American trip in 1969, but after that it was almost unknown in the capital for several years. It did appear at an exhibition at Kensington Olympia on 10-11 August 1974, and clocked up another notable feat by taking the exhibition train overnight to Carnforth afterwards, on routes on which steam was forbidden.

No 4472 also had a quick visit to the East End in November 1984, for a Royal Train, no less. On 20 November, for the official opening of North Woolwich station museum, No 4472 hauled a short Royal Train from Stratford, conveying the Queen Mother, who performed the opening ceremony. *Flying Scotsman* added to its fame by becoming the first preserved steam engine to haul a Royal Train on the main line.

Regular steam passenger trains at any London terminus simply did not happen for more than 15 years but eventually, in 1985, official sanction was given for steam to use Marylebone station.

The one-time terminus of the Great Central Railway's London extension was a quiet backwater compared with other London termini, but it had been a regular haunt of *Flying Scotsman* during the war and in the early 1950s, and in 1985 it could even still boast an operating turntable. First to break the new ground was *Flying Scotsman*'s Carnforth stablemate, A4 Pacific 4498 *Sir Nigel Gresley*, the great designer's 100th Pacific, named in his honour in a ceremony at Marylebone station in November 1937.

While at first it was enthusiasts' tours, often steam-hauled one-way, the plan was for a regular series of steam-hauled up-market dining trains to Stratford-upon-Avon, with a small fleet of engines stationed in the diesel multiple unit depot by the station.

Flying Scotsman moved to Marylebone in December 1985, and took its turn on 'Shakespeare Limited' trains to Stratford during the year, but in 1987, the engine found itself moving around the country to an unprecedented extent, still nominally based at Carnforth and working in the north of England, but also sometimes hauling trains from London, or in the Midlands, or even on the Southern Region between Salisbury and Yeovil, a route also recently opened up for steam.

At the end of 1987, though, *Flying Scotsman* moved south on a more permanent basis, not to Marylebone, but to be based at Southall in west London. This was to spell the end of its long association with Carnforth. Roland Kennington took over as the engine's chief engineer, and he immediately had a big job to do.

After being absent from the capital for many years, *Flying Scotsman*'s return to working trains out of London was apparently only going to be for a very brief period. It may have found a new home in west London, but that was not going to be its sphere of operation, at least not for the next 12 months or so…

Above left: During a then-rare visit to the Southern Region, *Flying Scotsman* stands alongside SR Merchant Navy Pacific No 35028 *Clan Line* at Salisbury on 6 June 1987.
BRIAN SHARPE

Above right: *Flying Scotsman* is turned on the turntable at Marylebone on 28 September 1986.
BRIAN SHARPE

Below: No 4472 leaves High Wycombe with a Santa Special returning to Marylebone on 3 January 1987.
BRIAN SHARPE

Above: Carrying the Stratford shed trademark of a Royal Train engine – a white cab roof – after hauling a train conveying the Queen Mother, No 4472 approaches Whittlesea on the morning of 24 November 1984, running light engine from March to Spalding, from where it would haul an excursion to Manchester.
BRIAN SHARPE

Right: Gresley's three best-known Pacifics line up at Marylebone in October 1986: *Flying Scotsman* is flanked by A4s Nos 4498 *Sir Nigel Gresley* and 4468 *Mallard*.
GEOFF SILCOCK

Scotsman goes to the

OUTBACK

Several British steam engines have been to North America, and a few have emigrated to Australia, but only one has ever visited America AND Australia.

1988 saw the bicentenary of the creation of Australia and, in true Aussie tradition, some major celebrations were called for. Quite apart from all the other parties, Aus Steam 88 was arguably the biggest steam spectacular staged anywhere in the world and, in recognition of the country's origins, it was felt that a famous British steam locomotive would add a certain something to the occasion. The Australians officially asked for *Mallard* from York Museum, but it was bad timing in that, although it happened to be in steamable condition, it was the 50th anniversary of its world speed record in 1988, and it was felt that *Mallard* ought really to stay in Britain.

However, it was a Melbourne postman who took the story forward. Walter Stuchberry was the chairman of the Aus Steam 88 committee and he was determined to get a famous British steam engine to the event. He asked Sir William McAlpine for *Flying Scotsman* instead and it was agreed, subject to financial guarantees, that No 4472 could attend.

Aus Steam 88 was very much a live steam event, centred on Melbourne, and engines travelled to it under their own steam, not just for exhibition but to haul trains in an intensive two-week programme of railtours.

Australia consists of six mainland states, and these are far more independent than might be expected, even to the extent of having largely separate railway systems, built to different gauges. New South Wales in the east adopted standard gauge. Victoria in the south and South Australia chose broad (5ft 3in) gauge, while Queensland and Northern Territories followed African tradition, with 3ft 6in gauge. In fact one-third of South Australian railways were built to 3'6" gauge. In recent years, there has been a programme of standardisation, with standard gauge track being extended from New South Wales, parallel with the broad gauge across Victoria to Melbourne, and parallel with 3ft 6in track to Brisbane in Queensland. The lines to Alice Springs, and across the Nullarbor Plain to Perth, have been converted to standard gauge a process completed in

1969. A bonus of having broad and standard gauge lines running parallel for hundreds of miles is that it is possible to run two steam trains alongside each other on parallel tracks, and the Australians frequently do.

Although *Flying Scotsman* was initially scheduled simply to sail to Melbourne, go on exhibition for two weeks and haul a couple of railtours, then stay on for a few months afterwards and work more tours from Melbourne and Sydney, there was potential for something rather more ambitious, potential that simply had not existed a few years earlier, before the spread of the standard gauge network.

Roland Kennington had overhauled the engine at Southall remarkably quickly, including the fitting of air-brake equipment; it had a run to Stratford-upon-Avon on one of the dining trains and was pronounced fit to emigrate, sailing from Tilbury on 11 September 1988 on the P&O container ship *New Zealand Pacific* via the Cape of Good Hope. While en route, a slight problem arose when the Port of Melbourne sold the only floating crane able to lift an A3 Pacific off the deck of a container ship, and *Flying Scotsman* had to be offloaded at Sydney instead on 16 October, just days before the start of the big party 300 miles away in Melbourne. No 4472 had to be steamed virtually the minute it touched Australian soil and, after a quick test run, set off on a two-day journey to Melbourne.

The Aus Steam 88 organisers had a cunning plan. Although *Flying Scotsman* was to be one of many steam engines on display in Melbourne, it was expected to be such a popular attraction that it was totally enclosed in a cocoon within Spencer Street station, and the public had to pay to go inside to see the Gresley Pacific. It worked, 130,000 people paid to see it and receipts during the two weeks virtually covered the engine's transport costs.

After Aus Steam 88, *Flying Scotsman* stayed in Australia to haul tours farther afield, back in New South Wales, working from Sydney, and then double-heading a 12-day Sydney-to-Brisbane tour using the new standard gauge line. Its partner was Australia's most famous Pacific, No 3801, a semi-streamlined engine that has itself visited most parts of the continent.

Scotsman was so popular and performing so well that it was agreed to extend its stay, and plans were formulated for even more ambitious outings. In August 1989, *Flying Scotsman* set out from Melbourne for the run to Alice Springs, the first steam engine to use the new standard gauge line. It was almost impossible not to break records, and No 4472 covered the desolate 422-mile stretch of outback from Parkes to Broken Hill, non-stop in nine-and-a-half hours, a world record for a non-stop run by a steam engine, beating its own record from 1928, which it had repeated in 1968. For the Australian run, two extra water 'gins' were coupled behind the tender, standard practice for Australian steam trains in a land with virtually no water. There

Above: *Flying Scotsman's* first railtour in Australia was from Melbourne to Albury and back on the standard gauge line across Victoria. The engine nears Broadford on 25 October 1988. BRIAN SHARPE were no half-full water troughs, fire hydrants or standby road tankers on the line to Alice Springs, and the engine simply had to haul sufficient water for the journey, as well as a heavy trainload of passengers and a diesel 'just in case'.

Flying Scotsman was not the only British steam engine in Australia, and in fact there was already another British express steam engine in operational condition. In 1925 it had stood next to *Flying Scotsman* at the Wembley Exhibition and claimed to be the most powerful steam engine in the world. In comparative

tests it had proved superior in many ways to *Flying Scotsman*, and many years later it had shared a shed with No 4472 in deepest Rutland. Now, though, *Flying Scotsman* was the star, and no one had thought it worthwhile moving *Pendennis Castle* across Australia for Aus Steam 88.

GWR 4-6-0 No 4079 had been sold to the Hammersley Iron Railway back in 1977 and was occasionally used for special trains on what is otherwise a totally heavy freight railway. The thought of reuniting the two British engines obviously occurred to a few

Above: Shortly after sunrise on 20 October 1988, No 4472 passes Culcairn in New South Wales, just south of Wagga Wagga, where the annual Eistedffod was being held. The engine is en route from Sydney to Melbourne for the Aus Steam 88 steam festival. BRIAN SHARPE

Right: The plaque commemorating the world record non-stop steam run remains on *Flying Scotsman*'s middle driving wheel splasher. BRIAN SHARPE

ON AUGUST 8TH 1989 THIS LOCOMOTIVE ACHIEVED THE WORLDS LONGEST NON-STOP RUN FOR STEAM TRACTION OF 422 MILES 759 CHAINS BETWEEN PARKES AND BROKEN HILL IN NEW SOUTH WALES AUSTRALIA

people. If *Flying Scotsman* could get to all the other state capitals, it could get to Perth. It would be a gigantic undertaking, even to move *Pendennis Castle* 1000 miles to Perth by road, but it was possible, and once a sponsor was found for the road transport, the reunion was on.

Flying Scotsman crossed the Nullarbor Plain, with its 299 miles of dead-straight track, becoming the first steam engine ever to cross the whole of Australia under its own steam, and on 17 September 1989, it came face-to-face with No 4079 at Perth. The two engines

embarked on a programme of tours in the area, sometimes double-heading, and sometimes hauling separate trains on parallel tracks, something that can be done in some areas, even on lines of the same gauge.

This was a fitting climax to a hugely successful tour of no less than 28,000 miles of virtually trouble-free running. If *Flying Scotsman* was not already the most famous steam locomotive in the world, it certainly was now!

The engine returned to the UK on the French vessel *Le Peruse*, from Sydney, this time via Cape Horn thereby circumnavigating the globe.

Above: No 4472 attracts large crowds at Albury on 25 October 1988, before returning to Melbourne.
BRIAN SHARPE

Left: GWR 4-6-0 No 4079 *Pendennis Castle,* then based at Hamersley Iron, comes face to face at Perth in September 1989 with No. 4472 *Flying Scotsman* during the latter's tour of Australia. The two first met at the British Empire Exhibition at Wembley in 1925, were once both owned by Sir Bill McAlpine, and both have now returned to Britain.
HUBERT DU GUESCLIN

Right round the
WORLD

No 4472 notched up another first while returning from Australia via Cape Horn, by becoming the first steam engine to circumnavigate the globe.

When *Flying Scotsman* returned from Australia, arriving on 14 December 1989, it was obviously tired from its exertions, but it still had a valid BR main line running certificate. It was soon back in action, and simply resumed a similar programme to the one it had left three years earlier, in marked contrast to its return from America almost 20 years earlier.

The main line certificate had only two years to run, though, and not only was consideration being given to the next major overhaul, but privatisation of British Railways was looming, and the future for main line steam operation looked more than a little uncertain.

In a slight departure from its normal sphere of operation, No 4472 even paid a working visit to a preserved steam railway, the Severn Valley, in September 1990. Prior to this, the engine's only serious runs on a preserved line were in 1973, when it had returned from America and been unable to run on the main line immediately, simply because it was summertime.

It is hard to believe that Gresley's A1s, when built, were almost too heavy, even for their own main line, yet in 1990, *Flying Scotsman* could run on a privately-owned ex-GWR branch line that would only have seen much smaller engines in real steam days.

Preserved steam operations have always centred on a boiler certificate for insurance purposes, which lasts for 10 years, after which a total strip-down, inspection and overhaul is compulsory. BR, though, imposed a shorter, seven-year limit on their main line certificate and, by

the 1980s, with weight restrictions being lifted, owners of main line engines were finding that, once their main line certificate had expired, they could run the engine for another three years on private heritage lines, to raise money for the next overhaul.

By 1992, this was even looking like a sensible option for *Flying Scotsman*. Many steam lines wanted it, believing it could be a big money-spinner, and for No 4472's owner it would see them through the approaching nightmare of privatisation, after which a decision could be taken on the engine's main line future. The seven-year main line certificate expired after a run to Stratford-upon-Avon on 25 October 1992.

**Above: Hauling
LNER Gresley teak
coaches again,
No 4472 departs from
Bridgnorth, during
its visit to the Severn
Valley Railway in
October 1990.**
PAUL STRATFORD

No 60103 runs on
HERITAGE
LINES

No 4472 retired from the main line on 25 October 1992 and almost immediately embarked on a tour of preserved lines, visiting the Great Central and East Lancashire railways as well as the Birmingham Railway Museum at Tyseley, where 'driver experience' courses were proving extremely popular – and what better than driving *Flying Scotsman*? Other railways were queueing up to hire the engine, among them the Llangollen Railway. No 4472 duly arrived and promptly failed with serious boiler problems.

Back in 1963, Alan Pegler had returned the engine to its single-chimney form, in LNER livery as he remembered it. It was never really an issue at the time as it was not called upon to run as fast or as economically as it had needed to do when in daily front-line express train haulage. After all, the single-chimneyed No 4472, still in low-pressure form as an A1, had officially broken the 100mph barrier in 1934, so in single-chimney A3 form as Doncaster had returned it to in 1963, it was still a good engine. It never reverted to being an A1, let alone a GNR-style A1 so, even in Pegler's day, it was a bit of a hybrid.

For those involved in running the engine, though, in later years, whose memories tended to be from the 1950s and 1960s, there was a desire to see *Flying Scotsman* as they remembered it, and in its optimum mechanical form, the fitting of the double chimney in 1958 having made a huge difference. Roland Kennington, in charge of No 4472, had been quietly collecting the parts necessary for the transformation, in the knowledge that he would struggle ever to get Sir Bill McAlpine's agreement to it.

The premature boiler failure at Llangollen meant that at least a boiler overhaul was necessary to keep the engine running, but the full main line overhaul was still not justified. This gave the opportunity for a surprise development in 1993, when *Flying Scotsman* appeared in its final BR condition as No 60103, in Brunswick green, with double chimney and Kylchap, and even smoke deflectors. It was the talk of the steam enthusiasts' world, even though most passengers were bitterly disappointed, many unable to believe that it was the real *Flying Scotsman* that was hauling their train.

McAlpine had agreed to it only until it could return to the main line. A double-chimneyed A3 could haul heavier trains more economically, but the transformed engine would run at 25mph, mostly on GWR branch lines, hauling six or seven coaches. The transformation took place with the assistance of Messrs Babcock Robey, who carried out the boiler overhaul, and No 60103 emerged from their works in July 1993.

Flying Scotsman immediately resumed its intensive programme of preserved line running, returning first to the Paignton & Dartmouth Steam Railway, although looking (and sounding) very different. This was followed by the Swanage, Gloucestershire Warwickshire, Llangollen, Nene Valley and Severn Valley railways.

It was while No 60103 was on its tour of heritage lines that a significant change of ownership occurred. It was rumoured that McAlpine sold half of *Flying Scotsman* to Pete Waterman, but this is not strictly true. McAlpine owned the operating company, known at various times as SLOA Railtours, Pullman-Rail and Flying Scotsman Services; its assets including Steamtown, the locomotive shed at Carnforth, as well as *Flying Scotsman* and assorted rolling stock.

In the run-up to privatisation, British Railways' train operations had been split into Inter-City, Regional Railways, Network SouthEast, Rail Express Systems and Railfreight. These became autonomous businesses, which were to be sold to the private sector. One other, smaller business, was the Special Trains Unit, which was a subsidiary of Inter-City and owned several sets of coaches used for special trains. Steam trains formed only a small part of this business, which also hired out its coaches for football specials, diesel railtours and any other special train working anywhere in Britain. When *Flying Scotsman* hauled a train up to October 1992, Flying Scotsman Services often hired the coaches from the Special Trains Unit who were responsible for running the train.

Now the Special Trains Unit, headed by David Ward, was for sale to a private investor. Well-known pop impresario and entrepreneur Pete Waterman bought it but, at the same time, McAlpine and Waterman agreed to merge their two companies. Now *Flying Scotsman* was the figurehead of all special train operations on the about-to-be-privatised railway system – except, of course, that it was not certified to run on the main line.

Nevertheless, there had been considerable investment in ensuring that there would be main line steam under the privatised regime and, with *Flying Scotsman* now effectively owned jointly by two extremely successful millionaire entrepreneurs, the future looked good.

Above: The nearest No 60103 got to the Great Northern main line was a couple of months on the Nene Valley Railway. *Flying Scotsman* leaves Wansford with a demonstration goods train on 8 July 1994, recalling the days when Gresley Pacifics hauled Anglo-Scottish fast freight trains.
BRIAN SHARPE

PRIVATISATION
of British Railways

Bitish Railways was privatised on 1 April 1994, but it was not a return to the pre-1923 situation of private companies owning trains and track. A new organisation, the late lamented Railtrack, owned the track and infrastructure and new Train Operating Companies (TOCs) were set up to operate train services, buying 'paths' on the system from Railtrack. Steam operations had previously come under the Inter-City banner, through their Special Trains Unit which dealt with all railtour and charter train operations, although it did not have a total monopoly and Network SouthEast and Regional Railways had occasionally run their own steam trains.

The politics of privatisation grew very complicated and messy and *Flying Scotsman*, without turning a wheel on the main line, was well-and-truly embroiled in the politics. Pete Waterman had become involved as there

Above: No 60103 *Flying Scotsman* on Berwyn Viaduct on the Llangollen Railway.
KEITH LANGSTON

was potential for new organisations to make money out of the newly-privatised railway system and Pete saw an opportunity not to be missed. He had bought the Inter-City Special Trains Unit and called it Waterman Railways and by owning all the rolling stock used on all railtour operations, this would give him a lucrative business, especially if he also owned some of the engines that would pull the trains. He had already achieved a minor miracle by getting a diesel locomotive passed by BR for main line operation at colossal expense, but no other diesel ever earned this accolade, and privately-owned diesels did not get a fair crack of the whip until privatisation.

Waterman Railways was never a TOC and its trains were operated by Res (Rail Express Systems) whose charging policies were causing problems for all tour operators.

The company went through some organisational changes with Flying Scotsman Railways becoming a new parent company, while Waterman Railways was the rolling-stock hire company, but access charges led to the company withdrawing from promoting its own trains. It would only hire trains to other railtour promoters.

Flying Scotsman failed again with boiler troubles at Llangollen and returned to Southall. With its 10-year certificate expiring shortly, it was now time for a decision as to whether to embark on the full main line overhaul. In view of the bad experience of the first months of Waterman Railway's operations, it was clear that the plans for *Flying Scotsman* to be the centre-piece of Waterman Railway's railtour operations, were not going to happen, as Waterman Railways no longer had any railtour operations of its own.

What if?

If Pete Waterman's plans had materialised, *Flying Scotsman* would probably have been overhauled to main line standards, possibly retaining its BR green livery and double chimney. It would have been a great success with many of Britain's steam enthusiasts, but, this would never have paid the bills, the overhaul would have cost a large seven-figure sum. Waterman is above all a businessman, and if the engine was not going to make money, it would not be part of his strategy. If, and it is a big if, it had been overhauled by him once to main line condition, it might have run for seven years, but would more probably have been sold. There is now a market for main line steam engines at the right price, and anything could have happened to the engine if Flying Scotsman Railways had sold it as a going concern.

The Engineer's
TALE

Geoff Courtney talks to Roland Kennington, *Scotsman's* chief engineer from 1986 to 2004.

There are several names which are synonymous with *Flying Scotsman*, particularly in its preserved, post-BR life. Roland Kennington is one of them.

Roland is the man who for nearly 20 years lovingly kept No 4472 going against what were at times overwhelming odds. Not for him, or his dedicated team of volunteers, warm and well-equipped premises, with an endless flow of money and a plethora of spare parts.

Instead he spent nearly two decades with the locomotive in dark, dank and cold sheds – and they don't get darker, danker or colder than Southall motive power depot on a January night – with clapped-out machinery, empty coffers, and a demanding public expecting the LNER legend to look and perform like a thoroughbred racehorse.

And he loved every emotionally-draining minute of it.

Roland was chief engineer for *Scotsman* from 1986, when Sir William McAlpine was the owner, until its sale by Flying Scotsman plc to the National Railway Museum in 2004.

His involvement resulted from one of the many mini-crises which have punctuated the locomotive's preservation history.

Just two days before Christmas in 1985 he received a telephone call at the Bedford engineering company WH Allen, for whom he was production manager. On the line was Ray Towell, the man in charge of No 4472 at Carnforth, where it was then based.

Ray had a problem that revolved around a broken combination lever, the Christmas holiday, and Sir William's 50th birthday.

"Basically the lever had snapped in two, on a test run up north, following an overhaul," said Roland. "It turned out the problem had been caused by a bolt being carelessly left in the motion during the overhaul.

"I had been working as a volunteer on A4 No 4498 *Sir Nigel Gresley* at Carnforth for the previous two years, so Ray thought of me when the problem arose.

"I told him the works was closing the following day for 10 days over Christmas, and he said something had to be done because the engine was needed for a special train early in January to mark Bill McAlpine's 50th birthday. The best I could offer was to weld the broken lever, which wasn't very satisfactory, but Ray eagerly agreed."

So the two parts of the lever were brought down from Carnforth by train to Milton Keynes and then taxi to Bedford – surely the cabbie's most unusual passenger over that festive period – and Roland welded the parts together.

"BR agreed to allow 4472 to run with the welded repair for two journeys only, but that was enough," said Roland. "Bill got his birthday train."

Four months later Roland took a call which was to literally change his life. "It was Bernard Staite, who worked for Bill and was in effect in charge of *Flying Scotsman*.

"He told me that Bill wanted to move the engine away from Carnforth and from the team that was then looking after it – I don't think the combination lever incident had done them any good – and place it in the care of a group of volunteers.

"Bernard said they were looking for an honorary chief engineer to head the group – note the word honorary – and my name had been mentioned. I was flabbergasted, and said there were two things to consider: firstly, I didn't know anything about steam engines, and secondly I needed to talk to my wife Chris."

The first consideration was no problem to Bernard or Bill, and the second was no impediment either. "Chris told me I'd do what I wanted whatever she said, and anyway she didn't mind. I decided I could fit it in with my full-time job at Allen's, so the next day I called Bernard and agreed to do it."

Roland said the Friday before he was due to start his honorary, voluntary position he went on a run with No 4472 and after its return to Marylebone, where it was then based, he overheard some traction inspectors

Left: Roland Kennington pauses briefly from his labours on *Flying Scotsman* inside Southall shed.
ROBIN JONES

talking about the testing of three-cylinder engines. "I thought to myself: 'You're out of your depth here, Roland.'"

But Roland wasn't out of his depth. "Without sounding big-headed I discovered I knew more than I thought, due largely to my 'apprenticeship' with *Sir Nigel Gresley*."

Having settled down into his role, events soon took another seismic shift. "Just before Christmas 1987 Bernard Staite told me that the state of Victoria wanted to borrow the locomotive as part of their celebrations to commemorate the Australian bi-centenary, and that if it happened he wanted me to accompany the engine.

"To be honest, I didn't think it would come off, but it did. It was initially for six months, and to my surprise Allen's agreed to release me, albeit without pay. However, Bill McAlpine knew the company's boss, and Bill got him to agree to continue paying my salary while I was in Australia."

That six months away from home turned out to be 13, with Roland flying to Australia in September 1988 and meeting No 4472 at Sydney where it arrived after six weeks on the high seas.

The highlight of No 4472's stay Down Under was undoubtedly the non-stop run on 8 August 1989 from Parkes to Broken Hill, a distance of 422 miles. The journey was accomplished in just under nine-and-a-half hours, with extra water being provided by three 7000-gallon water carriers – or water gins in Oz parlance – behind the corridor tender.

The run was the longest ever non-stop journey by a steam locomotive, a world record which stands to this day and almost certainly will never be beaten.

Back home towards the end of 1989, the scenario for both Roland and No 4472 took on a darker hue. "I was made redundant – Allen's probably thought that if they could without me for 13 months they could do without me for good – and money for the engine started running out."

Roland's outlook brightened up when he found work with another engineering company, but that for *Flying Scotsman* was gloomy and money became tight.

By 1993 pop impresario Pete Waterman was involved. He and Sir William each owned 50 per cent of the company, which in turn owned the locomotive, with Pete the chief executive.

"Bill let Pete run the company and he did what he liked," said Roland. "In 1993 the ticket for the main line ran out and private railways were invited to make bids for being loaned the engine. The result was a two-year programme on nine lines.

"This was a double-edged sword for me. I was out of a job by then, but was at least travelling around the country looking after the engine and getting my expenses paid, but at the same time everyone knew *Scotsman* was being beaten into the ground."

That beating took its toll, and the locomotive was eventually declared a non-runner on the Llangollen Railway, where it spent an ignominious spell out of steam with visitors 'cabbing' it at £1 a time.

Roland was to discover, however, that there is indeed a silver lining behind every cloud. "A story about the engine's condition was broadcast on the radio, and as a result the Midlands boilermaking firm Babcock's offered to restore the boiler, in return for publicity.

"Bill gratefully accepted, and as I had no job at the time he asked me to work with Babcock's. They made a new smokebox from BR drawings, and I grabbed the opportunity to fit a double chimney, which I had

wanted to do for a long time. Babcock's also made some smoke deflectors from original drawings."

After 10 weeks the work was done and the private railway programme continued, but the Bill McAlpine ownership period was nearing its end.

"The company which owned the engine was seriously in debt, and Bill took back control and in 1995 put the loco up for sale. This was picked up by one of the railway magazines, and soon after I got a call from Bill saying he had sold the engine – and me with it!"

It transpired that pharmaceutical entrepreneur Dr Tony Marchington had seen the article and agreed to meet Bill's £1.25-million price without even inspecting the engine, which by then was in a sorry state in Southall shed, its base for several years.

"I had never heard of Tony Marchington, so I rang him from a callbox on Waterloo Station to introduce myself," said Roland. "I arranged to meet him at Southall, where he would see for the first time something for which he had paid more than £1-million!"

Tony immediately sanctioned a rebuild of the sorry-looking *Flying Scotsman*, a job which was to take three years and cost not far short of another £1-million.

"I was elated," said Roland. "It meant I was going to be able to do something I had wanted for years – turn a mediocre locomotive into the equivalent of an A4. Tony wanted a 'Rolls-Royce' job, and I was determined to give it to him."

And a Rolls-Royce job it certainly was. On 4 July 1999 *Flying Scotsman* made a triumphant return to the main line, when an estimated million people lined the route from London to York.

The engine looked absolutely gorgeous in apple green and carrying the number 4472, and there was more than a few tears as youngsters and adults alike cheered and waved the mighty locomotive and feted its crew.

"For the first two years of Tony's ownership everything went well," recalled Roland. "The engine was very busy, and there was great interest everywhere we went. But then money became tight and I used every trick to keep it running, although it never ran in an unsafe condition.

"We had to be ingenious at times."

Ingenuity wasn't enough, however, and after travails which have been well documented No 4472 was once again put up for sale.

In sharp contrast to that under Sir William McAlpine, this sale was carried out in the full glare of the public and media, with the National Railway Museum mounting an overt and unabashed publicity campaign aimed at securing the locomotive 'for the nation' while private individuals were also beavering away in the background.

Eventually the NRM won the day, paying £2.1-million plus buyer's premium.

"There was a certain amount of inevitability about the NRM getting the engine," said Roland. "I was disappointed. I readily accept that all good things come to an end, but I do not think it should have gone to such an organisation or have been bought with Lottery money – I think it should have stayed in private hands.

"That's not sour grapes, but I guess that is how it may sound."

No Roland, it doesn't. After 18 years of dedication to *Flying Scotsman* which went way beyond the call of duty, you have a right to say how you feel. Every anorak, every enthusiast, and every member of the public who will in future enjoy this LNER masterpiece, is in your debt.

Top: Its LNER apple green livery having been applied at the 11th hour, the reborn' No. 4472 *Flying Scotsman* - complete with double chimney - proudly stands at King's Cross on the morning of Sunday 4 July 1999 while passengers board the historic 'Inaugural Scotsman train to York to mark its comeback.
ROBIN JONES

Above right: Dr Tony Marchington with his prize possession minutes before its departure to York.
ROBIN JONES

Right: Clear road ahead and we're off! *Flying Scotsman* departs from Kings Cross at 8.55am on 4 July. ROBIN JONES

BOUGHT
by another millionaire

Flying Scotsman's tour of heritage lines came to an abrupt end on 23 April 1995, when it was withdrawn from service with boiler troubles, again while at Llangollen.

The 'dream team' of McAlpine and Waterman could have been good for Flying Scotsman under different circumstances, but both seemed to agree that the engine needed more money spending on it than either was prepared to invest. Its earning potential simply did not appear to be sufficient to justify the expenditure required. For the first time since 1972 in America, Scotsman was in limbo, its future very uncertain.

It needed another owner and that person came along in the larger-than-life figure of Dr Tony Marchington, proprietor of Oxford Molecular Group plc, a company with a value estimated at £200-million. In February 1996, Dr Marchington bought Flying Scotsman Railways, including the engine and all the company's other assets – which included a set of Pullman cars but not Waterman Railways – for £1.25-million, and embarked on probably the most thorough and certainly the most expensive overhaul ever carried out on a British steam engine.

Roland Kennington. who had been the engine's chief engineer since 1986 and who knew it inside-out, remained in charge, with the work being carried out in the one-time GWR locomotive shed at Southall.

It was a job that was to take more than four years, the plan being that, on completion, Flying Scotsman would undertake an intensive series of up-market premium-priced dining trains for wealthy customers all over Britain. Marchington invested part of his considerable private fortune in the project. A team of financial experts was assembled and the future looked rosy, although steam enthusiasts recognised that No 4472 was no longer part of their scene, as the engine's future trips would be aimed at a totally different price range, way beyond their means.

1995 had seen a very significant development when SR Bulleid Merchant Navy class Pacific No 35028 Clan Line had emerged from an overhaul fitted with air brakes, making it the first steam engine to be able to haul the premier luxury train, the Venice-Simplon Orient Express. This had proved to be a great success, and Marchington and his team felt that the market was big enough for another similar operation, but with the added attraction of Britain's most famous steam engine always at the head.

Costs escalated, though; first the Pullman cars were sold. When Flying Scotsman did appear in the summer of 1999, it would have to haul stock hired from elsewhere, with a consequent effect on profits.

The overhaul was not just thorough, it amounted to a total rebuild into what was, in effect, a non-streamlined A4, with the boiler, which was from an A4 anyway, uprated to a pressure of 250psi, and the cylinders rebored. Flying Scotsman was more powerful than ever, still fitted with its double chimney and, in a major departure from previous practice, it was not only fitted with air brakes but it had its vacuum braking system removed.

It carried LNER apple green livery though as No 4472, making it completely unacceptable as an authentically preserved locomotive.

But this was not the idea; the engine had to earn its keep, and the instantly recognisable livery and number was part of the marketing plan, while the design enhancements would make it capable of hauling heavy trains anywhere.

Just as when No 4472 disappeared to America and returned to a totally different world, completely different circumstances greeted No 4472 on its return from the wilderness this time: the brave new world of privatisation.

The main plank of privatisation was open access; Railtrack could not simply enforce arbitrary rules as to what could run where. If it was practicable, it was permitted and, since 1994, steam had been allowed not only on 25kv electrified routes, but all of the major inter-city ones at that.

For maximum impact and publicity, Scotsman's debut in its new guise was to be between King's Cross and York, the line it had been built for 76 years earlier, and on most of which it had not been seen for 30 years. Whatever may have gone wrong with the sums, this was a triumphant return, beyond what anyone could have imagined.

The timescale was tight, the engine was only just completed and run-in on time, and a little paintwork remained unfinished, but its performance was fantastic, and the public interest was colossal. An estimated one-million people lined the route to see the engine's return – just what the company needed.

Venice-Simplon
ORIENT EXPRESS

nfortunately, it is probably fair to say that financially at least, it was mostly downhill from then on. When the engine ran, it was like no other, certainly not like any other A3 Pacific, but although most of its trains did sell, there were not enough of them. Privatisation, which had opened up the routes it needed to run on, especially out of the main London termini, also led to the well-publicised backlog of maintenance of the railway system, making it almost impossible to plan tours because large chunks of the system, while theoretically open to all, were, in fact, shut to all for maintenance.

A major problem became the East Coast Main Line as *Flying Scotsman*'s route, King's Cross to York, was just too popular with the travelling public, and an extra train, travelling at half the speeds of the GNER expresses, simply could not be fitted in at the time it needed to run. Wealthy clientele, having paid several hundred pounds for a ticket to ride behind the world's most famous steam locomotive, did not want to sit in Retford down goods loop for an hour, waiting for a slight lull in the traffic.

The plan to overhaul A4 Pacific No 60019 *Bittern*, also acquired by Marchington, was abandoned and the engine sold. Marchington had also bought back what was left of *Flying Scotsman*'s second tender, which had been sold to the A1 Trust, who were building a brand-new LNER Peppercorn A1 Pacific. The project to rebuild the second tender also fell by the wayside.

A problem found with the engine during its first winter of main line operation with a double chimney was that of drifting smoke obscuring the driver's vision. Just as BR had fitted smoke defectors to cure this problem (eventually), the decision was made to refit them towards the end of 1999. The engine was now very definitely 'non-authentic' in appearance, carrying 1958-style double chimney and 1962-style smoke deflectors, but turned out in pre-1939 LNER apple green livery.

Other organisers hired *Flying Scotsman* – one even ran it from St Pancras to Inverness – but they were soon disenchanted by the nightmare of dealing with the bureaucracy of the privatised railway system. Two things kept *Flying Scotsman* going: the unerring commitment of Roland Kennington and his team, and a potentially lucrative contract to haul the 'Orient Express'.

The VSOE was launched in 1984 as a luxury train running a couple of times a week from London to Venice. The train ran in two parts, Victoria to Folkestone and Boulogne to Venice or other European destinations – using superbly restored vintage Pullman cars in Britain and Wagon-Lits dining and sleeping cars on the Continent. Passengers used the ferry to cross the Channel.

Gradually an increasing programme of domestic tours was introduced so that the public could experience travel on Britain's most luxurious train, not cheaply, but without the expense of going to Venice and flying back. There had always been thoughts that steam haulage would be a considerable added attraction on the domestic runs, but the fact that the train was air-braked only, to be compatible with the modern railway system, while steam engines are traditionally vacuum-braked only, made it impracticable until 1995.

The SR Merchant Navy Pacific *Clan Line* proved to be a big hit on the VSOE and the operators and passengers liked having steam on the front of the train. *Flying Scotsman* managed to pick up a piece of the action, on an occasional basis at first, from August 2000, and then as the preferred engine when Clan Line retired for its next seven-year overhaul. VSOE runs generally started from Victoria, and ran to destinations such as Southampton, Bath, Worcester or Stratford, although occasionally No 4472 ran from King's Cross to York or vice versa. VSOE also introduced the 'Northern Belle', offering a similar standard of luxury, albeit in less-interesting coaches, for customers in northern cities. *Scotsman* took its turn on this train, sometimes to Scarborough, but often between York and Newcastle.

THE PEOPLE'S ENGINE

Tony Marchington had always intended to launch a public limited company so that individuals could buy shares in the engine. That way it would not be owned by an individual, and its future well-being would be assured. The VSOE contract with a guaranteed income from 30-40 trains per year was what the company needed to make it attractive to investors. Flying Scotsman plc was launched on Ofex, the junior stock exchange, on 3 December 2001.

Individuals could now buy a share in the *Flying Scotsman* name, and initial interest from the public was described as massive, with eventually more than £1.3-million being raised. One investor who bought a small stake in the engine was none other than Alan Pegler, who had saved it from being scrapped in 1963.

But *Flying Scotsman* still had major problems. Tony Marchington antagonised VSOE management by taking his engine to a traction engine rally in Derbyshire, making it unavailable for several of its contracted jobs. He had first taken it to Hartington Moor rally in 1999 after a bet in a pub. There were times when there was simply insufficient money for simple running repairs to get *Scotsman* fit for its next VSOE duty, and the A3 was also a little oversized for trips in Kent, where the VSOE often runs to.

Sea Containers Ltd, owners of the VSOE, looked forward to the return of *Clan Line*, and also signed up a couple of other air-braked Bulleid Pacifics to cover for the A3. It is probably also fair to say that, to make money, *Flying Scotsman* had to make more runs per year on VSOE trips than the largely volunteer support crew was physically capable of.

Nevertheless, when it was good, it was very good; the VSOE is a very heavy train and the A3 worked harder than it ever had in its previous 80 years' service, turning out power beyond anything even Gresley could have dreamed of. Impressive though its power output was, it actually added little to *Flying Scotsman*'s fame as far as the great British public was concerned. After the initial flurry of interest shown by the media and the public in 1999, little was heard of the engine on its travels, except for occasional rumours about its financial situation and its long-term future.

Top: *Flying Scotsman* **leaves Dalwhinnie on the Highland main line with a Holland & Holland St Pancras-to-Inverness special on 19 October 2000.** JOHN SHUTTLEWORTH

Left: No 4472 visited Peak Rail at Matlock in August 2000 and attracted 20,000 people. JEFF COLLEDGE

The Director's
TALE

Geoff Courtney talks to David Ward, former operations director of Flying Scotsman plc

David Ward and *Flying Scotsman* go back a long way – more than half-a-century, in fact. A railwayman all his working life, David joined the newly fledged British Railways in 1948, based in York. "*Scotsman* was, of course, a regular visitor then, passing through on East Coast Main Line expresses, and I saw it on numerous occasions," he recalled.

"Even then there was something about the locomotive – the name is brilliant, very charismatic. Its reputation and public perception was then, of course, also enhanced by the fact that there was also this romantic train, 'The Flying Scotsman'.

"The public often confused the two, and I suspect still do."

As David progressed through the BR ranks, No 60103 – as it was in BR days – continued plying its trade on East Coast metals until the men in grey suits decided in 1963 that its time had come. The engine was, it seemed, destined for the cutter's merciless torch, leaving behind just memories and a record or two.

Alan Pegler, though, had different ideas, and in what was probably the most publicised public salvation of modern times, he bought the locomotive seemingly from under the scrap dealers' noses.

"I have complete admiration for Alan and what he did, but in all honesty the railway historians have not portrayed the complete picture," said David. "It wasn't really a case of either Alan buying or *Scotsman* being scrapped.

"There were others in the field, trying to find the money to buy the locomotive, but Alan was a member of the BR Eastern Region board and was able – quite understandably – to pull a few strings."

By this time David Ward was based in Norwich, and No 4472 – as it had become in preservation – was a regular visitor to that cathedral city, running specials in the twilight of BR steam.

When that twilight turned to total darkness in August 1968, Alan was allowed to continue running *Flying Scotsman* on the main line under an agreement with BR. This deal was to run until 1971, and meant No 4472 was exempt from the ban that applied to every other steam locomotive. Even early in its preserved life, No 4472 was blazing trails.

At this point David Ward became involved with the locomotive for the first time from a formal operational point of view. "A number of people were nominated by BR to liaise with Alan over the running of his special trains, and I was one of them."

Flying Scotsman continued its high-flying career – visiting both the United States and, some years later, Australia – and so did David Ward, who was appointed

Director Special Trains in 1984.

In this role he was responsible for all non-timetabled trains, which included Royal, VIP and heritage trains involving steam, diesel or electric traction. Once again No 4472 was within his remit.

In 1994 David retired after a 46-year railway career, but two years later 'the world's most famous steam locomotive' was once again to become a part of his life – only this time in a big, big way.

"I received a call from Roland Kennington, who was chief engineer for *Flying Scotsman*," explained David. "He told me a Dr Tony Marchington had bought the locomotive, and asked if I would be interested in looking after the operational side.

"Roland told me a little about Tony, and said that he had bought the engine to put something back into the community. He also told me Tony wanted a 'Rolls-Royce' overhaul, and that there was no problem with money.

"I was interested, so I went to see Tony at the headquarters of his pharmaceutical company in Oxford. I had come from a very different world, from a nationalised industry where money was tight and everything disciplined. I took Tony at his word and felt his intentions were sound, so I agreed to become operations director."

With the overhaul completed in 1999, David's days as a retired pensioner were put on the back burner. He was about to enter a new phase in his business life – albeit one that was unpaid – that must have come as a total shock to someone who had spent his entire career in the warm, polarised and orderly embrace of BR.

It is to his credit, though, that he adapted to such an unaccustomed environment with aplomb, showing a talent that probably surprised no one who knew him but a fighting spirit that raised a few eyebrows.

The people with whom he worked within the *Flying Scotsman* circle were an eclectic bunch of individuals who probably had only one thing in common: their lives were about to revolve to varying degrees around an elderly 160-ton lady who demanded constant attention.

They included a steam locomotive owner who tended to get his own way whatever that way may be, a chief executive who was a qualified solicitor and former Conservative MP, a chief engineer whose knowledge of the locomotive was probably greater than any other living person, and a PR man whose motor industry background was about as far removed from the strait-jacketed world of BR as it was possible to get.

David's disagreements with the chief executive – Peter Butler – and the PR man were legion. He would become frustrated at what he perceived as a lack of knowledge on the subject, irritated by an attitude that to him bordered on excessive laissez-faire, and bewildered when a problem that to him was of vital importance wasn't treated with the same reverence by others within the circle.

He accepted, for example, that there was enormous and boundless public and Press interest in the locomotive, but failed to see why linesiders and people waiting at stations – none of whom had contributed in any way to saving the engine or keeping it running – should be allowed a free spectacle.

On one run to Lincoln, for example, the PR man had arranged to broadcast live from the train via his mobile telephone to the local radio station, reporting on progress at regular intervals as they approached the city. Such was the public enthusiasm whipped up by this exercise that a crowd estimated at 10,000 was waiting at the station and by the line as *Scotsman* drew in.

The PR chap was beside himself with delight as he saw a sea of excited faces thronging the platform, with not an inch of space unoccupied. To him it was a job well done. David was appalled, genuinely feeling those people had no right to enjoy the sight or get in the way of the passengers who had paid a tidy sum to be on board. It was, he said, a 'fiasco'.

Despite such disagreements, however, David was the ultimate professional, bringing to the party much-needed expertise and a veritable tome of contacts that played their part in keeping the show on the road. He was, arguably, the man who stitched everything together, and he seemed never to resent waking up to yet another problem.

It was an extremely busy period, for Tony Marchington and Peter Butler were determined that No 4472 should travel far and wide, reaching such geographically diverse towns and cities as Norwich, Yeovil, Plymouth, Shrewsbury, York and Inverness. As operations director David had his hands full, and insiders will tell you that he personally never let anyone down.

The financial jinx that is so woven into the locomotive's preservation history began to rear its debilitating head, however.

"Early on, Tony had a vision of running a first-class outfit," said David. "He had bought another locomotive – A4 No 60019 *Bittern* – owned a set of Pullman cars, and was also interested in buying a set of sleeping cars. It could have been a very good business, but unfortunately the capital wasn't there. It went downhill in terms of aspiration and the vision.

"Things were OK for a couple of years, but then I began spending a lot of time trying to keep the operation afloat. Suppliers were on stop, and financially we never knew where we stood."

The company had a contract with the Venice Simplon Orient Express luxury train operation but this, too, had its problems.

"I remember that once we had to pull out of providing *Scotsman* for three VSOE trains, which meant a loss of £12,000 income – and all for a repair that would have cost £2000. It was all a struggle and very depressing."

In another well-publicised episode, No 4472 was unavailable to the VSOE because Tony wanted it to appear at a country steam fair he was involved with.

"The thing I regretted most was letting the VSOE people down, whatever the reason. They were an excellent company to deal with, and I hated making the call giving them the bad news.

"My allegiance was always to *Flying Scotsman* and not the people who were running it. What went on was doing the name of the locomotive no good at all."

Knowing so intimately the locomotive's financial travails, it could hardly have been a surprise to him when it was announced early in 2004 that *Flying Scotsman* was for sale.

However, as with chief engineer Roland Kennington, with whom he forged a close and rewarding business relationship, he had his misgivings about its purchase by the National Railway Museum.

"I think it was wrong to spend public money when private finance was available. Three private owners kept the locomotive operational for 41 years and 445,000 miles – that is a record to be proud of.

"When *Flying Scotsman* was handed over to the NRM it was in a far better condition than when Tony Marchington bought it eight years earlier and, indeed, was probably in its best condition since being withdrawn in 1963. You have to give him credit for that."

FOR SALE
world-famous steam engine

There was no solution to *Flying Scotsman's* financial problems; the company made a trading loss of almost £500,000 in 2002. Over £2-million had been spent on purchasing and overhauling the engine, but much of this was in the form of bank loans. Marchington was, on paper, a multi-millionaire, but his fortune was linked to the value of his company, Oxford Molecular Group plc.

The management team at Flying Scotsman plc expected to command big city salaries, and the cost of running the company far exceeded the income generated by the engine. No 4472 had a value, but it had to be estimated at around £2.5-million in order to keep the company solvent, but no one was actually likely to buy it at that price just to clear the company's debts and overdrafts.

A solution was to sell the rights to the name *Flying Scotsman*, an asset registered in the name of the company, to an investor who could use it for financial gain. A shopping centre called the Flying Scotsman theme park, steam village or even shopping mall was one particular brainchild, and it was to be built in the Peak District, or perhaps Doncaster, or even Edinburgh…

The idea was that a consortium building a shopping centre for billions of pounds could call it the Flying Scotsman Shopping Centre on payment of a couple of million pounds to Flying Scotsman plc, and the use of the name would add much more than a couple of million to the value of the finished item. It was never clear whether the engine itself was part of the deal, and at best it seems an over-estimation of the value of the name *Flying Scotsman*, famous though it is.

Marchington's involvement ended in July 2003 with his resignation from the board, and he was, in fact, declared bankrupt in October, although not exclusively because of *Flying Scotsman*. The financial problems of Flying Scotsman plc simply compounded the problem of the collapse of the share price of Oxford Molecular Group plc.

If it had not been for Dr Marchington, *Flying Scotsman* may never have been overhauled to main line condition again. The plans for the engine at the outset were perfectly realistic, but the overhaul cost so much that the engine simply could not earn sufficient income to pay the interest on the bank loans taken out to pay for it. Few main line steam engines make sufficient money to cover the cost of a seven-year overhaul, and many are paid for with help from the Heritage Lottery Fund.

On 3 November 2003, Ofex suspended trading in the shares of Flying Scotsman plc.

With No 4472 still making regular VSOE appearances, the situation degenerated into farce when the engine was advertised for sale in 2003 by a used car dealer. True, he was a dealer in very expensive vintage vehicles, even if his premises resembled a barn used for rearing hens. An end to this chapter in *Flying Scotsman's* history was clearly approaching, but what might happen to it now?

Top left: No 4472 stands at its birthplace, Doncaster Works, on 26 July 2003. An open weekend was held to celebrate the works' 150th anniversary. The engine received a full professional repaint in exchange for its guest appearance. BRIAN SHARPE

Far left: *Flying Scotsman* at Hartington Moor traction engine rally in June 2002. PAUL STRATFORD

Left: The Motor Shed – home to classic car dealer Malcolm C Elder, whose circular claimed that he had been asked to 'discreetly' offer *Flying Scotsman* for sale. PHIL MARSH

Save our
SCOTSMAN

With it becoming increasingly inevitable that *Flying Scotsman* would be sold again, considerable public debate ensued. Fortunately, though, it was not all just talk, and serious moves were afoot to raise the money needed to purchase it so that it would remain in Britain and remain in steam.

The management of Flying Scotsman plc still considered they had an asset worth a considerable sum, and were determined to see it sold for an amount that would clear all the debts of the company. What was clearly important to the company was to ensure there were several bidders, and if this included overseas collectors, then so be it.

Among the rumour and counter-rumour it was stated that the National Railway Museum would like to acquire it, and not just for display as a static exhibit. Jeremy Hosking, owner of A4 Pacific No 60019 *Bittern*, was interested, but not at any price. A Midlands-based businessman also emerged as a serious bidder, and there

continued to be rumours that overseas investors were interested.

At the time, Flying Scotsman plc was still trading and the engine was still running. It was in serious debt to its bank, and therefore could not sell the asset for less than its market value, and this could only really be established by offering it for sale by tender. The sale was officially announced on 16 February 2004, with a deadline of 2 April for receipt of sealed bids.

Within three days, the National Railway Museum launched its Save Our Scotsman campaign, aimed at raising sufficient money to be assured of obtaining the engine. This meant it had to be sure of exceeding the bids of unknown potential purchasers, and offering sufficient to satisfy the company's creditors, primarily the bank. It was at this stage that it became apparent just how famous the engine was, and how much the British public cared about it, as £365,000 was raised from public donations within the first five weeks, a level of support unprecedented in the history of steam preservation.

Above: Unfortunately not in steam, *Flying Scotsman* still broke the tape declaring Railfest 2004 at York open on May 29, and made its triumphant arrival at its new permanent home, even though being pushed by a diesel.
ROBIN JONES

It was without doubt one of the most incredible and successful fundraising initiatives ever staged by a state-owned British museum, to acquire a historic artefact for the nation.

The museum's campaign was supported by MPs across the country, companies such as GNER, which operate trains on 'the route of the Flying Scotsman', local newspapers such as the *Yorkshire Post*, and perhaps most notably, Sir Richard Branson, head of Virgin Trains, who offered to match pound-for-pound the amount donated by the public. The museum also made an application to the National Heritage Memorial Fund, the parent body of the Heritage Lottery Fund, for emergency funding; an amount of £1.8-million being agreed.

What caused the huge upsurge in public interest and support? Was it the threat of the engine disappearing overseas forever? Or was it the fact that *Flying Scotsman* had simply not existed for almost 10 years as far as most people north of London were concerned anyway? After a period out of use and a long-running overhaul, it had hauled expensive up-market trains, mainly south and west of London in recent years.

Perhaps the public were really saying 'we want our engine back', to pull trains for ordinary people in all parts of Britain. Certainly they did not just say so, they put their money where their mouths were.

It was publicly announced on 19 April that the National Railway Museum's bid of £2.31-million had been successful. At least one other bid came close to this figure, but the engine was now in public ownership; finally a part of the National Collection, thanks to the NRM's initiative, public donations, the NHMF and all the individuals and companies that had lent their support.

Now it was safe, and a new chapter in the engine's history was about to unfold.

The National Railway Museum bought the engine to run it, and its arrival at York was timed to coincide with

Railfest, a week-long celebration at the end of May 2004, of the 200th anniversary of Trevithick's Penydarren tramway locomotive, and the centenary of *City of Truro*'s 100mph run in 1904.

No 4472 would arrive at York hauling a special train from Doncaster conveying invited guests. It was a high-profile media occasion and, although the engine ran light from Southall as far as Doncaster, it was found to have a leaking boiler tube on arrival and was unable to haul the train, having to be towed to York and pushed into the exhibition site by a diesel. Not a good start!

Above: Launching the Save Our Scotsman appeal at York station are, left to right, Hugh Bayley MP, GNER chief operating officer Jonathan Metcalfe and NRM head Andrew Scott. NRM

Left: Sir Richard Branson celebrates the saving of *Scotsman* **with one of several bottles of bubbly.** NRM / PA

Above: Pupils of Inglebrook School hand over their pocket money to the NRM's head of education, Julia Fielding, in the museum's Great Hall.
NRM

Above right: At Railfest 2004 at the National Railway Museum are Sir Richard Branson and Alan Pegler, who had first saved *Flying Scotsman* from being scrapped in 1963.
ROBIN JONES

The Scarborough
FLYER

Although *Flying Scotsman* could not steam when it arrived at York, it was not a major repair job, and the museum was confident in advertising trains from York to Scarborough during the summer, to be hauled by its famous new acquisition. Interest in these trains, running twice a day, three times a week at just £25 for the 84-mile round-trip, was enormous, with 1000 tickets sold on the first day they were on sale.

On the first day of service, 20 July, there were some shunting problems in actually getting the engine and its train into the platform ready for departure, and *Scotsman* was over an hour late. As it pulled in to platform five, though, it was greeted by a spontaneous round of applause. When did any other steam engine ever earn that?

Unfortunately, *Flying Scotsman* broke down several more times during the summer, often with the eyes of the media watching it. They were relatively minor problems, and quite quickly repaired, but disappointing for the new owners and for the travelling public.

The 42-mile line from York to Scarborough was opened by the North Eastern Railway in 1845. The line leaves the East Coast Main Line at the north end of York station, and immediately crosses the River Ouse. The line runs in a fairly straight line through Haxby and Strensall, but approaching Kirkham Abbey, the line twists and turns alongside the River Derwent, before reaching Malton. From here, there were once branches to the north to Pilmoor and a line heading south to Driffield. Now only the Scarborough line remains, and a few miles beyond Malton is the site of Rillington Junction, where the line to Pickering and Whitby diverged to the north, before its closure in 1965. The Pickering to Grosmont section is now the North Yorkshire Moors Railway,

but the nine-mile section south of Pickering was lifted.

After another straight, level stretch, the line from Hull joins at Seamer Junction, on the outskirts of Scarborough. Just before the terminus is the derelict platform at Londesborough Road, used for excursion traffic in steam days, and near it was once the locomotive shed, where the turntable was reinstated in 1980. The line from here to Whitby, also closed in 1965, dives into a tunnel just before the station, and all trains had to reverse to use this line, an unusual and inconvenient arrangement.

Although Scarborough had its direct express from King's Cross in steam days; the 'Scarborough Flyer', it was never hauled by a Pacific north of York, so the use of *Flying Scotsman*, and often other Pacifics on this route is something that has only happened in the preservation era.

Above: *Flying Scotsman* **prepares to depart from York on 20 July 2004 with its first train to Scarborough since being purchased by the National Railway Museum.** BRIAN SHARPE

Left: Arrival at the destination of Scarborough is an event in itself. The Town Crier is on hand to greet the engine. JEFF COLLEDGE

Scotsman's partner, a bird called
BITTERN

One of the real Cinderellas of British steam preservation is LNER A4 streamlined Pacific No 60019 *Bittern*. No less than six of Gresley's 35 A4s have been preserved, against just the one A3. Of the A4s, two are in North America, *Mallard* is in the National Collection, *Sir Nigel Gresley* was bought by a preservation society and *Union of South Africa*, by an individual, John Cameron, and these last two have been maintained in almost continuous main line service.

The sixth is *Bittern*, which was bought by an individual, Geoff Drury, along with the last surviving A2 No 60532 *Blue Peter*. *Bittern* was purchased in working order in 1966, later restored to LNER blue as No 19 and was on the original list of BR-approved steam engines allowed to operate after 1972. It ran just twice, to Scarborough.

Meanwhile *Blue Peter*, being unique and, like *Flying Scotsman*, having a marketable name with public appeal (also named after a racehorse, not the TV programme) received rather more of its owner's attention. Despite this, it was 1992 before *Blue Peter* hauled a main line train in preservation, and only after a society, the North Eastern Locomotive

Preservation Group, had assumed responsibility for its operation and overhauled it. The NELPG also took over *Bittern* in the deal with Drury, but it was considered almost unrestorable, so it was cosmetically restored (as LNER No 2509 *Silver Link*) and displayed at various venues.

Eventually the Great Central Railway had started to dismantle it with a view to returning it to steam when Tony Marchington stepped in. He bought the engine from Drury, and had every intention of operating it as *Flying Scotsman's* partner. When Marchington's plans started to fall apart, *Bittern* was the first casualty. Jeremy Hosking bought it from him, and is quietly restoring it at Ropley on the Mid-Hants Railway. Jeremy Hosking is the millionaire enthusiast who restores engines because he can, not necessarily to earn a profit on his investment.

Hosking's millions are real, not just on paper and subject to the vagaries of the stock market. If *Flying Scotsman* had been available at the right time at the right price, Hosking might well have acquired it instead of, or as well as *Bittern*. Would he have made a success of it, or would it have ruined him? We do not know, but we shall see shortly what success he has with *Bittern*.

What if?

When *Flying Scotsman* was sold to Tony Marchington, it was in a condition such that it would not undertake any more main line running without several hundred thousand pounds being spent on it. Three years of preserved line running, with only essential running maintenance following a boiler overhaul, when only the work necessary to run on private lines at 25mph had been done, had left the A3 almost beyond economic repair.

The engine had, for three years, done jobs it just was not designed for, and that had more of an effect on its well-being than anyone could have predicted. It was like using a Ferrari just to go to the corner shop.

So the economics were stacked against it; it could not justify any major expenditure if it could not hope to recover that expenditure. But at least it kept running, even if restricted to 25mph mostly on ex-GWR branch lines. Everyone concerned deserves great credit for not just keeping the engine running, but running it in probably its most intensive period of use since withdrawal by BR, in very difficult and uncertain times.

Undoubtedly more people had the pleasure of a ride on the *Flying Scotsman* in the early 1990s than in any other period; many even had the honour of driving it.

But *Scotsman's* only real hope of long-term salvation was a multi-millionaire enthusiast who, unlike Pete Waterman, did not expect quickly to recoup every penny he spent on it, plus interest. If Tony Marchington had not bought it, then it must be a reasonably safe bet that, within a few years, Jeremy Hosking would have done.

In the
WORKS

lying Scotsman had a major rebuild in 1995-1999 at a cost of around £800,000. It remained main line certified throughout the ensuing five years, but covered a relatively low mileage in view of some long periods not being used, mainly because of shortages of money. It had never actually broken down while hauling a train during its period working for Flying Scotsman Railways, mainly on Orient Express duties.

It was reasonable to assume, therefore, that it was in fairly good condition and, with two years left on its main line boiler certificate, the National Railway Museum decided to keep it running, and not to carry out a full overhaul until the certificate expired in 2006. The public had supported the appeal and it was only reasonable to make the engine available for the public to ride behind as quickly and as often as possible. To have immediately stripped it down and for it not to be on public view for a couple of years was not really an option.

Unfortunately a series of relatively minor breakdowns conspired to make No 4472 available for only some of its planned Scarborough runs. There was no question of letting it loose on any more ambitious main line runs, or hiring it to any heritage lines. Once the first season of main line runs was over, the engine went straight into the museum's workshops for some quite extensive remedial work. It unfortunately missed another high-profile run in September, when it had been scheduled to haul a train conveying the Prime Minister, Tony Blair, to the opening of Locomotion: the National Railway Museum at Shildon, in the PM's Sedgefield constituency.

The price paid for the engine in 2004, although a lot of money, left enough in the kitty to finance the engine's ongoing maintenance, and the Scarborough runs had made a small profit. A cash injection from Yorkshire Forward, for a permanent exhibition at York based around the engine, and to assist in its mechanical upkeep, also helps to keep No 4472's bank balance healthy.

It was basically considered fit to run at the end of the 2004 summer, and not in need of an immediate major overhaul. However, there were a number of fairly major jobs required, to ensure a more reliable level of performance in the summer of 2005. The museum has a policy of carrying out maintenance not only in-house, but in full view of the public. Despite being in a fairly heavily dismantled state for the next nine months, No 4472 remained on view and was a major attraction in the museum.

Jim Rees, rail vehicle collections manager at the National Railway Museum, explains: "When the engine arrived, it could best be described as tired. Yes, it had been putting up terrific performances hauling loads beyond what was expected during its BR service, but it is an A3, fitted with an A4 boiler running at A4 pressure of 250psi. Gresley had not designed the mechanics of the A3 to handle this kind of power and it was having an effect on the engine."

There was a crack in one of the cylinders that had to be repaired, and the engine needed a complete piston and valve examination and overhaul. Much work also centred on the boiler. On its arrival at York, Jim immediately reduced the working boiler pressure to 220psi, but it was some time before the condition of the boiler could be established. York water is relatively clean and, after a while, the condition, particularly of the crown stays, became more evident.

A major programme was undertaken to replace many of these stays, which hold the top of the firebox to the inside of the boiler. Replacing many of them can then result in additional stresses on adjoining ones, which subsequently also need replacing.

There were other minor problems with plumbing on the engine, particularly relating to the air brake system. All these jobs were attended to, in the expectation of a higher level of reliability in the second season.

Above: No 4472 in the works, partly dismantled, but on public display.

Below: In the works.

Ride the
LEGEND

Above: *Flying Scotsman* **departs from York on 17 August 2005 with the 6.10pm to Scarborough.**
BRIAN SHARPE

Above: *Flying Scotsman* **departs from York on 17 August 2005 with the 6.10pm to Scarborough.**
BRIAN SHARPE

Above right: *Scotsman* **brings its train into York to pick up another trainload of satisfied customers.**
BRIAN SHARPE

Right: No 4472 departs from Scarborough on 31 May, early in the second season of trips to the seaside.
BRIAN SHARPE

The timescale for the work on No 4472 was very tight, but the engine was ready for the 2005 season. The public had clearly forgiven its indiscretions the previous summer and advance ticket sales were phenomenal. For the first couple of days in Spring Bank Holiday week, it delighted its public with its runs to the seaside. Volunteer supporters working on the train reported a carnival atmosphere on board, such was the relief that No 4472 was finally back in tip-top condition.

Even in the first week, though, problems arose with the boiler, and *Scotsman* failed to appear on the third day. It was repaired in time for the start of the main season, though, and Thursday 7 July was the 160th anniversary of the opening of the line to Scarborough, with major celebrations planned around *Scotsman*'s runs that day. In view of the horrific events in London that morning, the celebrations were cancelled as a mark of respect but, in any case, on arrival back at York on the previous day, there were more boiler problems with *Flying Scotsman* that would take two weeks to repair.

In the meantime, 'Hogwarts Castle' stood in for a

week, but the passengers were not impressed. There were reports of people travelling hundreds or thousands of miles for the ride, and bursting into tears when *Scotsman* failed to show. 'Hogwarts Castle' may be famous, but it is not a 'real' engine and, in any case, Warner Brothers, distributors of the Harry Potter films, do not allow the engine to run as 'Hogwarts Castle' in public service, and it carries its *Olton Hall* nameplates.

For the following week, *Scotsman*'s smaller sister, V2 2-6-2 No 60800 *Green Arrow*, was ready to take over instead and again ran for two days quite satisfactorily, although it was still not what the passengers wanted. On the Thursday, though, *Green Arrow*'s middle big-end fractured near Scarborough, causing considerable damage to the engine that will be costly to repair. The following week, boiler repairs completed, *Flying Scotsman* was back in business.

But what should be a routine steam trip to the seaside was turning into a nightmare for everyone concerned for the second year running, and *Flying Scotsman* was starting to become the most famous steam engine in the world for all the wrong reasons.

It went from bad to worse again after a couple of days. No 4472 was on its way back to York on the morning trip when an unattended rucksack was spotted on the station platform at York, by a coffee bar. The station was evacuated and the police called in the Army from Catterick, who carried out a controlled explosion.

Meanwhile, *Flying Scotsman* with its trainload of passengers had been brought to a stand just outside York station and stood for over two-and-a-half hours. The evening train was cancelled, passengers from Scarborough were stranded in York and some from York were stranded in Scarborough. To top it all, further problems were found with *Scotsman*'s boiler, and Ian Riley's LMS 'Black Five' 4-6-0 No 45407 *The Lancashire Fusilier* had to stand in for a few days.

Although the run from York to Scarborough is one of the easiest jobs a large main line steam engine can be asked to do, it is 42 miles of level track, with a 60mph speed limit throughout. After a lifetime of breaking speed, endurance and haulage records with comparatively few mechanical problems, it could be said that the most famous steam engine in the world should find the jaunt to Scarborough easy.

But the engine is 82 years old – the second-oldest running on the main line in 2005. While other main line steam engines now make on average a dozen runs a year, such is the public demand for the most famous one of all that *Flying Scotsman* is expected to run three days a week for a three-month period – and that is far harder work, for the engine and its operators, than is expected of any of its younger competitors.

By the end of the 2005 season, the operation was judged to be successful and *Flying Scotsman* was immediately on its way to Crewe Works (hauling some of the museum's diesels) to take part in The Great Gathering open weekend.

Back to
THE FUTURE

Above: The A3 boiler carried by *Flying Scotsman* from 1978 to 1995, which is being rebuilt by Riley & Son Engineering and will be replaced on the engine during the current overhaul. BRIAN SHARPE

Right: The stewards from the NRM 'Ride the Legend' trains, present the train manager, Tracey Parkinson, with a Thank You gift on the morning of *Flying Scotsmans* last run of the season on 8 September. NRM

The National Railway Museum completed its historic purchase of *Flying Scotsman* on behalf of the nation in the spring of 2004, and Jim Rees assumed responsibility for the ongoing preservation and operation of the engine.

Just as it was important to clarify why Alan Pegler had bought it in 1963, so it seemed appropriate to understand why the latest (and last) purchaser has now bought it.

The answer is quite simple really: "This is the largest railway museum in the world and *Flying Scotsman* is the world's most famous steam engine."

But Jim Rees adds: "It became clear during the fundraising campaign that most people, both the public and the media, were amazed to find that the museum did not, in fact, already own it."

Jim was never under any illusions that it was going to

be east, and it has been a hard slog. Just like Alan Pegler more than 40 years earlier, the museum did not just buy the engine to preserve it, or to stop it being scrapped or sold abroad. The engine is the public's favourite, and there is overwhelming demand for it to run. There is absolutely no thought of the engine being 'stuffed and mounted' in the foreseeable future.

He said: "We bought it to keep it running. The engine was mechanically very tired when it arrived, but the main problems were with the boiler. The first thing we did was to immediately reduce the boiler pressure to 220psi, as the A3s were designed to run at that.

"Another early problem to address was that the engine did not own a chimney. When the last A3, No 60041 *Salmon Trout*, was scrapped in 1966, a chap bought its chimney. Many years later, Roland Kennington had found out about it, borrowed it and put it on the engine when it had its rebuild to double-chimney condition in 1993. But it never actually changed hands, so we had to negotiate to buy it from the chap who owned it."

Jim added: "People think we could just put the old single chimney back on; they don't realize that there is a big difference inside the smokebox between a double-chimney A3 and a single-chimney one."

Has the engine made money since the museum bought it? "There has been a small surplus on the operation so far, despite us having had to carry out more running maintenance and repairs than had been hoped for."

Again, like Alan Pegler so many years earlier, the museum did not expect to make money out of the engine. The problem over the past two summers has been to balance expenditure on essential repairs to keep the engine going and investment in its long-term future. It has two boilers. The one it carries in 2005 is an A4 one, last carried by No 60019 *Bittern* in 1965, which was bought by Alan Pegler as a spare. It was fitted to the engine at an overhaul in 1978. The other is an A3 boiler that was carried by A3 No 60041 *Salmon Trout*, but removed in 1963, three years before it was scrapped. This boiler was fitted to No 4472 when it was overhauled at Darlington in 1964 after Pegler had bought it.

The A3 boiler, not used since 1978, is now the better of the two, and has already been sent to the works of Riley & Son Engineering at Bury 'for a major rebuild, not just an overhaul, which will make it fit for the next 20 years at least'. This will speed up the engine's return to service, and make it more of an authentic A3.

"But our problem," said Jim, "is that, having decided that the present boiler is never likely to see further service, we have not wanted to spend money on repairing it during the last two years, other than necessary running maintenance."

Coincidentally, Alan Pegler bought the cylinders from *Salmon Trout* when it was scrapped. The middle one was fitted during the Marchington overhaul. The museum will fit one of the outside ones, so *Flying Scotsman* will run with *Salmon Trout's* one-time boiler,

Brian Sharpe meets Jim Rees, rail vehicle collections manager at the National Railway Museum at York

chimney and two of its cylinders.

How much will the overhaul cost? Jim's estimate is £600,000. He knows the engine well by now and does not expect any surprises. The money is available, boosted by a Lottery grant, and a recent and very welcome donation of £75,000 from GNER, which advertise their East Coast Main Line expresses as running on 'The Route of the Flying Scotsman'.

The boiler has gone to Bury already. The engine, after its appearance at The Great Gathering at Crewe Works, moved on to the Tyseley Locomotive Works at Birmingham, from where it will haul a series of dining trains to Didcot before Christmas. Then it will return to The Works at the museum for the overhaul to start. The target for completion is August 2007. This is a very tight timescale, especially as the work will be done by the museum's engineering staff of just three. Some other work as well as the boiler will be sub-contracted out.

The museum readily admits that it wants a more reliable engine. The aim is to have an engine in August 2007 'which will do everything an A3 should do, nothing more and nothing less. It has no records to break and nothing to prove'.

There is one obvious and so far unanswered question. Will it be a single-chimneyed or double-chimneyed A3?

"The jury is still out on that one," said Jim.

The museum bought the engine to run it, so performance and reliability is an important issue, perhaps uniquely in the case of this one engine in the collection. It does not need to haul the heavy trains it hauled in its VSOE days, and the A3s were not built to climb hills, but the double chimney and Kylchap transformed the engine's performance in the 1950s. *Flying Scotsman* ran far more economically in its second season at York, but it also surprised everyone by continuing to steam one day even when a superheater element came apart from the header. This was a major problem, yet the engine carried on, something it probably could not have done in single-chimney form.

When there is a desire to run the engine, not just to Scarborough, but over the Settle & Carlisle line, and hopefully even from King's Cross to Edinburgh occasionally, the advantage of the double chimney cannot be disregarded. There is a strong argument that a museum is responsible for conserving an item in exactly the condition in which it obtained it, but perhaps the strongest argument is the simple fact that there simply is not an A3 single chimney and blastpipe available to fit to the engine.

Nevertheless, there are also compelling arguments for reverting to the single chimney, as this is the form that the public recognise. Because many of its followers in Yorkshire had not seen the engine for so long, many believe that it is the museum that has fitted the smoke deflectors, and they want them removed.

Jim actually tried running it to Scarborough without deflectors, but admits to being surprised as to what difference it made. Even in summer, and only running at above 40mph for parts of the journey, the lack of smoke deflectors does cause visibility problems on a double-chimneyed engine. Even so, it may be possible to run occasionally without them, if only on the Scarborough run.

So a decision has yet to be made on the issue of the chimney, and time is running out. The museum's collections committee will make the decision in the fairly near future.

Jim points out one feature that will definitely please the purists, though, and points to the corner of his office. "There is a proper, fully-working A3 whistle in that cupboard."

The whistle carried by No 4472 was wearing out, and not really loud enough, and was replaced by Roland Kennington with a much louder chime whistle a few years ago.

The engine will remain on view during its overhaul, but there will also be a permanent 'Flying Scotsman' exhibition at the museum. This will relate to the train and, while No 4472 may occasionally be part of the exhibition, it will be equally valid for the Stirling Single or a Deltic diesel to feature. It should help to clear up that continuing confusion between *Flying Scotsman* the engine and 'The Flying Scotsman' the train.

"*Flying Scotsman* is the most famous steam engine in the world, and it is still continuing to become more famous," said Jim.

However, he feels that further overseas exploits are unlikely, and have not actually contributed much to the engine's following in Britain. The engine has undoubtedly diverted management and staff time and effort since the museum bought it, but he is adamant that the engine will continue to run, because the management and staff at the museum are absolutely committed to it. "They all WANT to keep it going!"

Long may the legend steam on!

Above: *Flying Scotsman* **will continue to run well in to the future under the National Railway Museum's custody.**
BRIAN SHARPE